So much to celebrate

Living out the Church year in the family

Tony Castle

First published in 2000 by
KEVIN MAYHEW LTD
Buxhall
Stowmarket
Suffolk IP14 3BW

© 2000 Tony Castle

The right of Tony Castle to be identified as the author of this work has been asserted by him in accordance with the Copyright, Designs and Patents Act 1988.

All rights reserved. No part of this publication may be reproduced, stored in a retrieval system, or transmitted, in any form or by any means, electronic, mechanical, photocopying, recording or otherwise, without the prior written permission of the publisher.

Previously published as *Let's Celebrate*
Hodder & Stoughton, 1984

Scripture quotations are taken from the Holy Bible, New International Version, copyright © 1973, 1978, 1984, by International Bible Society. Used by permission of Hodder & Stoughton Ltd. All rights reserved.

0 1 2 3 4 5 6 7 8 9

ISBN 1 84003 554 4
Catalogue No 1500356

Illustrated by Angela Palfrey
Cover design by Jonathan Stroulger
Typesetting by Richard Weaver
Printed and bound in Great Britain

Contents

FOREWORD	5
INTRODUCTION	7
CHAPTER 1 **Advent** – The Coming of Love	9
CHAPTER 2 **Christmas and Epiphany** – The Showing of Love	27
CHAPTER 3 **Lent and Holy Week** – The Offering of Love	41
CHAPTER 4 **Easter** – The Triumph of Love	65
CHAPTER 5 **Pentecost** – The Giving of Love	81
CHAPTER 6 **Time after Pentecost** – The Living of Love	95
INDEX	109

Dedicated to
John, Theresa, Joseph and Katie

Foreword

Tony Castle opens this book in the kitchen: the centre of any home. The 'celebrations' that he describes, and encourages families to try, are intended to nourish the spiritual life of those in the home.

What particularly appeals to me is that this is not just another book on family prayer, but a book that brings the prayer at the heart of the Church and its worship right into the home, giving even the youngest members of a family access to its teaching and truth.

This is an important book because we live in an age when children are exposed more than ever to the world of unbelief, with its lack of values and standards. So many children and young people suffer from over-stimulation and have never learned the value of sharing in a creative activity with the rest of the family or a few moments' pause of prayerful silence together.

This book will help parents and guardians to remedy that, and create an atmosphere where children are encouraged to learn about the deeper meaning of life, and, together with their parents, to seek, to know and to respond to God. If you are a parent or a guardian who needs help with this, that help is now at hand.

Delia Smith

INTRODUCTION

The ideal family does not exist. Since we are each unique individuals, made in the image of God (Genesis 1:27), each family is going to be uniquely different from every other family. Some families are very musical, some are very artistic; others again are sporty and practical, while others have reading and study as a central interest. For whatever reason, some families are led by one parent, while other families are struggling in an area of great unemployment. No two families are the same; no two families have identically the same skills within them or the same needs.

It would be an almost perfect Christian family who, year after year, used all the following suggestions for celebrations in the home. Many, but not all, of them have been used, at one time or another, in my own family; some are regular favourites in friends' families. This book was put together, in captured moments, in a very noisy and busy family of four young children; with the additional and constant presence of the children my wife minds during the day.

Kitchen tables are not the focal points they once were, but I have found that ours serves as a very unifying presence in the home. Apart from sitting round it, as often as we can, to share a family meal together, children draw, colour and paint on it; grandmothers sit at it, to transmit gossip and impart advice; familiar visitors share a coffee and the local news at it and so on.

While the meal table is the natural gathering point for the family, the altar table in our local church is the focal point for the family of God each weekend. That weekly gathering, to share the word of God and the sacrificial meal, is to recall and celebrate the first Easter. Although the purpose of this book is to help families understand and celebrate all the seasons and festivals of the Church's year, the reader will find that one event is constantly referred to, directly and indirectly, an event which overshadows every other day in the year: the resurrection of the Lord. No other event demonstrates so vividly or dramatically the immeasurable love of Jesus; no other event shows more clearly the re-creation work of the Father and the Holy Spirit. It is *the* event upon which the whole of our Christian Faith is founded: 'And if Christ has not been raised, our preaching is useless and so is your faith' (1 Corinthians 15:14).

Many years ago, when Pope John Paul II visited Britain, he mentioned the family several times in his homilies. At York he said:

> 'I urge that your homes be centres of prayer; homes where families are at ease in the presence of God.'

At Wembley stadium he said:

> 'May your homes become schools of prayer for both parents and children.'

Impossible ideals? They would seem so to some, but if we do not have high ideals and standards to aim for, even if we fall short and do not attain them, we will just sink into mediocre indifference. Humans need targets. This book offers very practical help to every Christian family that believes that it is important to try to come closer to Christ through the celebration of the Christian seasons and feast days.

I would like to draw attention to what this book is not. It is not intended to be read from cover to cover, but rather to be dipped into. For example, at the beginning of Advent or Lent parents might like to read the appropriate chapter, looking for suitable ways for them to enliven the season in their home. Some of what they read might be put into action at once, while other ideas the family might have to 'grow' towards, little by little, as time passes.

The very first edition of this book appeared as *Let's Celebrate* in 1984; the American edition was published the following year as *Family Celebrations*. This new, updated and enlarged book has adopted the title *So Much to Celebrate*.

I would like to thank Delia Smith for her continued interest in this book and Sally Brierley for helping to get it ready for publication.

Tony Castle

Chapter 1
ADVENT
The Coming of Love

Introductory thoughts

'Hurry up, we'll be late!'
'I'll have to run if I'm going to catch the bus!'
'Peter's got to be at his music lesson at six;
   Chris has got ballet at six-thirty.'

We are creatures ruled by time. We 'take' it, 'save' it, 'spend' it, 'waste' it. Time moves relentlessly on with measured pace; yet when we are happy it seems to fly and when we are miserable it appears to drag. This ancient little verse can be seen in Chester cathedral:

> When I was a child I laughed and wept – time crept.
> When as a youth I dreamed and talked – time walked.
> When I became a full-grown man – time ran.
> And later as I older grew – time flew.
> Soon I shall find while travelling on – time gone.
> Will Christ have saved my soul by then? Amen.

Time limits us

It is often said that 'time is money'. Much more serious than that, time is life. For as the minutes tick by we become progressively older; our lives tick by. To use time well is to live our lives well, to waste time is to waste that which is most precious of all to us, our lives.

Occasionally we stop and look at our children, or find an old photo of them, and then we realise how they have grown. With that realisation comes the thought that we too are getting older. When we in turn look at our parents (if they are still with us) we see what time is doing to them. We are sadly reminded of the shortness of life and how limiting it is.

God has no limits. He's very lucky. He doesn't grow old. Minutes, hours, days, weeks, months, even hundreds of passing years have no effect upon him. He is outside time. We start a new calendar year on 1 January. It has meaning for us, but not for God. Every day is NOW for him. We start a new Church year with the first Sunday of Advent, but still it has no effect upon God. It is still NOW for him. Even the Church's holy seasons do not do anything to or for God. The Church's year is for our benefit, to help us draw closer in love and service to the Father, through the Son by the power of the Holy Spirit.

Gloucester cathedral has a sundial with these words on it:

Give God thy heart, thy service and thy gold;
The day wears on and time is waxing old.

Time started when God decided to create; before that there was no time. The motion of God's creation, the sun, planets, and the earth with its moon, makes time. The moment God said, 'Let there be light,' time began and has flowed on ever since. The twelve months of our calendar, from January to December, measure that time.

The Church's year, however, begins not in January, but with 'the coming' or 'Advent', as it is called. It is a title that implies a passing of time, a period of expectation and hope. It is the season of the Church's year which is most concerned with 'time'.

Love is God

Just as we can't talk about 'the year' without speaking about 'time', so we can't think about 'the family' and family life without considering 'love'. And that word is probably the most used and abused in the English language:

- the child says, 'I love bananas'
- the romantic novel tells us of 'the love in her eyes'
- the Jewish proverb says, 'Love your neighbour, even when he plays the trombone'

- the husband says to his wife, 'I love you'
- the Apostle John tells us that 'God is love'.

Surely the greatest revelation of the Good News from Jesus was this, that 'God is love' (1 John 4:16).

Genuine human love is a share, in some mysterious and wonderful way, in that love which *is* God. For example, when a couple fall in love and have that 'swept-off-your-feet' experience, they are immersed in a love which is a share in God's love. Assuming a couple want to express this love in the gift of themselves to one another in marriage, they move even closer to God when they make that commitment. It is the beginning of a life of commitments in and through the family. And God is continually looking for such expressions of love from us: 'If you love me,' Jesus said, in John's Gospel, 'you will do what I ask' (John 15:10). Marriage is a total commitment in love.

Love made visible

The loving gift of one person to another, helping the marriage to grow in maturity, can produce the visible sign and expression of their love – the new baby. Pope John Paul II has called the family 'a community of love'. It is a community that starts with a 'falling-in-love' and grows to maturity through the physical sexual expression of that love.

There is a saying that goes, 'A baby is God's sign that he wants his world to continue'. God did not stop creating the world; he goes on and on, every minute of every day, expressing his love in time, through the love of parents for one another. Parents work with God in the passing on of life. They are co-creators with God – God needs loving parents. Love is absolutely essential for each of us. Unless there is a loving atmosphere in which the child can learn to receive and give love he will never grow to full and proper maturity.

Some years ago the following story appeared in one of our national newspapers:

Kevin, a 10-year-old from the country, came to spend the Easter holidays with his aunt who lived in the London suburb of Wimbledon. Curious to explore not only her large garden but also an overgrown path at the back, he heard odd noises coming from a shed in a neighbour's garden. When he asked his aunt about the noise she told him that she thought her single lady neighbour kept chickens. Kevin had been brought up on a chicken farm and knew immediately that what he had heard was not 'chicken noise'. He went back through a hole in the fence to investigate. The neighbouring garden was very overgrown but with a clear path running from the house to the old shed. The shed door was padlocked and the window was blacked out, but there was a large sort of letter-box slit in the door. First checking that no one was watching, Kevin tried to peep through the 'letter-box'. It was covered on the inside by a piece of hanging material, but a powerful stench caught Kevin's nose. Just as he was about to give up and turn away the cover was lifted and a pair of wild staring eyes appeared at the slit. Kevin gave a startled scream and bolted out of the garden back to his aunt's. He ran straight into her. He was so upset that he blurted out just what he had seen. His aunt called the police.

The dignified maiden lady was very indignant at first when the police asked to inspect her garden shed. When they insisted, her resistance collapsed and she gave them a key. With some difficulty they opened the shed door and a sight met the eyes of the two constables that they are never likely to forget. Cowering in a darkened corner from the bright light and the frightening intruders was a naked figure of what appeared to be a strange animal. It was on all fours and had long black hair. There was terror in the wild eyes and 'it' emitted shrieks of panic. The police officers, taken aback by the sight, and the stench, closed the door again and radioed for assistance.

The 9-year-old boy was taken into very special care. He had been in the shed for seven years, since the age of 2, when the woman, fearing discovery of her secret illegitimate child, had incarcerated him in the shed, which he had never left. Besides the filth, long hair and nails, his back was bent in such a way that he would never be able to learn to walk upright. Terrified at the presence of other people, he could not communicate but merely expressed emotions by grunts. He had never known any caring love and there was no hope of a return to full human existence.

This extreme case shows most dramatically what happens to a work of God's creation if there is no caring love, and if there are no parents, or parent, to give time to teaching a child how to walk, how to speak and how to learn from play and family example. The less love there is in a human's life the more like an animal that person becomes; the more genuine unselfish love there is, the nearer the person comes to God. Without caring love children cannot grow to full maturity.

God steps into time
At one specific moment in history there was a great meeting between 'Time' and 'Love' and the result was a weak, helpless baby. When God came into our world that is how he came. On the first Christmas night the Son of God, 'Love' itself, became one of us.
We need to prepare carefully for our annual celebration of that great event.

ADVENT

The 'coming season'
In the Church's season of 'the coming', we find not just one meeting of 'Love' and 'Time' prepared for and celebrated, but three. The liturgy of Advent speaks of the three 'comings' of Jesus. This can be a little confusing, unless clearly spelt out and thought about:

1. The coming of 'Love' as a baby – the first coming of Jesus as a member of a human family.

2. The coming of 'Love' as the Word of God – the second coming of Jesus at the age of 30 as a preacher.
3. The coming of 'Love' as the judge – the final coming of Christ at the end of time as our judge.

In the four weeks of Advent these three 'comings' of Jesus are recalled. It is a time to consider their importance for us.

In family life so much is learned in a cumulative way by the constant repetition of advice or a good habit or practice. That is the way children learn how to behave. It is the same in the family of the Church. The Church's year, like Nature's seasons, comes round again and again. We do not need to be anxious about doing and learning everything at once. The repetition has an effect and the influence builds up over the years. How then can we best use the time of Advent to grow in knowledge and love of God? Here are a number of practical suggestions.

Practical suggestions

Advent resolutions

A new year, a new beginning and an ideal opportunity to make a fresh start or at least a special effort.

If giving time to our children is a mark of our love for them, so too giving time to God is an expression of love. For centuries Christians have used Advent and Lent to make a renewed effort at building a closer relationship with Christ. Simple, not-too-difficult-to-fulfil resolutions help to keep the family on course for a more satisfying celebration of Our Lord's birthday and all that it implies for us. If prayer has been neglected in the family, now is the chance to make a new start; if some of the following ideas seem attractive and feasible, now is the opportunity to introduce a few of them (more can be added next time Advent comes round!).

But beware! During the season of Advent the commercial world is trying hard to 'sell' Christmas to the shopper. Their interest in Christmas starts long before Advent begins and closes with the shops on Christmas Eve. For us, that is when

Advent ends and we *begin* to celebrate Christmas, a celebration that runs on until 6 January and the feast of the Epiphany. In some traditions it continues until Candlemas, the Presentation of the Lord, on 2 February.

Advent calendar

Of all the aids to mark the 'coming' feature of this religious season, the Advent calendar is the best known and most widely used. While these calendars with their step-by-step approach to Christmas have become more and more popular, most of those for sale in the shops have lost their original meaning and purpose. To be a proper 'coming' calendar it should count off the days to the Christ child's birth with a growing sense of wonder and excitement. The overall picture, before the little windows are opened, should not be of Father Christmas or a Walt Disney character; nor should it be of a nativity scene. The first two have no immediate connection with Advent, and the second totally destroys the sense of 'coming'. The scene should unfold gradually, with only the final picture revealing the true meaning of Christmas.

From Switzerland has come the notion of having pieces of chocolate hidden behind each 'window'. These calendars, despite appeals from younger members of the family, should be avoided at all costs; they totally destroy the aim and object of the 'coming' calendar. (Such calendars are often 'raided' and despoiled long before the end of Advent.)

The ideal calendar will have, for example, an overall picture of a village scene – Bethlehem – with people going about their everyday work. (Avoid glitter and tinsel pictures because they give the wrong impression. There was no glitter about Christ's birth; he came into a very ordinary village scene.) As the 'windows' are opened more and more of the life of the village is revealed, until finally, on 24 December, the nativity scene is revealed.

Once a good Advent calendar has been found it can be used over and over again, as long as the windows have not been torn out and can be folded back.

The children should take turns in opening the different windows on the calendar. Breakfast is a good time for this. It is an ideal opportunity for one of the parents to say just a word or two (nothing more, otherwise it gets 'boring') about a scene on the calendar, perhaps pointing out how long the Jewish people had waited for the Messiah. The parent might explain that life was going on as usual in Bethlehem, even though the Son of God was to be born there.

Some children love making Advent calendars and an enterprising family might, well before Advent, make it a family project.

Note that, for convenience, Advent calendars begin on 1 December. In reality Advent often begins two or three days before that, four Sundays before 25 December, so the calendar does *not* begin on the first day of Advent.

Advent wreath

In Ancient Greece wreaths were hung by young people on their lover's door as a sign of affection. Throughout history they have regularly been used to signify honour and joy. An Advent wreath is more than a decorative wreath of holly leaves, evergreens and berries. In addition it has four candles standing upright and representing the four Sundays, or weeks, of Advent.

The wreath can be hung by ribbons, for example from a light fixture in the middle of the room, or it can more safely be placed on a side table or on the dining room table.

Wreaths can be constructed in various ways. Here are a few suggestions that might help.

1. This is probably the simplest method. Cut out a circle of cardboard about 8 inches (20 cm) in diameter (you can get one out of a large cornflakes or cereal packet), make a 2-inch hole in the centre and cover it with silver cooking-foil. Give it a thick edge of evergreen, holly, ivy, etc., which can be attached through the cardboard with fuse wire. A few little red bows can be added to give a dash of colour. Four large mounds of modelling clay, or Blu-Tack, are

placed at equal distances apart on the inside edge, into which to push the four red or purple candles. If desired, symbols can be fashioned out of white pipe-cleaners (see page 21 on the Advent House and Jesse Tree) and placed in turn, each week, flat in the centre. (*This wreath is not suitable for hanging.*)

2. Two old wire coat hangers are very useful for the foundation of a larger, more solid wreath. Pull the bottom straight lengths out until they are bowed, then lap them over one another, so that the top of each hook just touches the 'bow' of the other hanger (see illustration). Now wire them together with fuse wire. Cover the frame with a strip of material (strips from a redundant sheet, perhaps), then a circle of evergreen. Fit candle-holders made from screw-on bottle tops into the four angles made by the overlapping hangers. Decorate with little red bows or suitable artificial flowers.

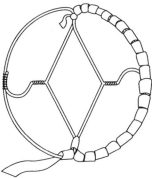

3. A substantial wreath can be constructed from a circle of wire netting (the sort that is used for rabbit hutches). The candle-holders can be forced into the already existing holes which, of course, can also hold the evergreen.

4. It is possible to purchase advent wreaths made of wire or styrofoam, which already have candle-holders attached and only require decorating with candles and greenery.

The Advent wreath is rich in symbolism which can be explained step by step to the children as they help make it.

The circle is a symbol of eternity – time without end. As you can go round and round the circle, without coming to an end, so time with God goes on and on. This is the never-endingness of God.

Evergreens stand for eternal life, life without end, because they don't die in the winter. In the same way God is always fresh and new; he never withers and dies. And we were born to live for ever with him.

Candles remind us of Christ, the 'Light of the world'. We are also reminded of the big candle at church, blessed during the Easter Vigil; small ones were given to us at our baptism. A writer in the early years of Christianity, Tertullian, said of Christians: 'You are a light of the world; a tree evergreen.'

Four candles represent the four weeks of Advent. Each Sunday we light a new candle as the celebration of Christ's coming gets ever nearer. (*Beware:* with children around, lit candles should never be left unattended.)

Perhaps the best way to use the Advent wreath is as a centrepiece table decoration, lighting a candle before, during or after the grace before Sunday dinner, when the whole family is present. (If the wreath is hung up somewhere in the house, it is not so accessible to the children.) The candles can be lit every day at dinner, but be sure to have a spare set of candles on hand, otherwise the end of Advent will arrive with only one or two stubs of candles left! Children love lighting candles and, of course, need to be supervised with care – they also like blowing them out! Everyone, except very young children, should get a turn lighting the candles and extinguishing them. (There are ten 'lightings' so there is plenty of opportunity for all.) If possible, the grace before the meal should mention the coming of Christ. As the Sunday's candle is lit, the person lighting it can say, 'Come, Lord Jesus, the Light of the world', or 'The Light of Christ'.

Advent candle

Instead of the calendar or wreath it is possible to make or buy a large candle with the numbers 1-24 running down the side of it. This too can best be used as a table decoration and lit at the principal meal each day. For its symbolism to have any value, the lighting of the candle each day should be accompanied by a prayer, perhaps as above.

The 'O' prayers

In the Church liturgy special sung prayers, called antiphons, have played a part for many centuries in the preparation for Christmas. They were called the great 'O' antiphons because each one began with an 'O'. Beginning on 17 December the ancient Old Testament titles of the coming Messiah are used in this prayer of the Church.

- The first addresses the Word of God as, 'O Wisdom' *(O Sapientia)*.
- The second title links up with Moses *(O Adonai)*, 'O Lord of Lords'.
- The third refers to Jesse, who was the father of King David. Of course Jesus was of the House of David and born in David's town of Bethlehem: 'O Root of Jesse' *(O Radix Jesse)*.
- The next antiphon uses the title 'Key of David' *(O Clavis David)* and refers to the kingly authority associated with David.
- The next one, 'O Rising Dawn' *(O Oriens)* speaks of the coming Messiah as the Light of the world.
- The antiphon for 22 December, *'O Rex Gentium'* (King of Nations), stresses that the Messiah is not for the Jews alone, but the whole human race.
- The final antiphon, *'O Emmanuel'*, uses the very special title which describes most exactly the role of the expected Messiah, 'God-with-us'.

The 'coming' season reaches a beautiful climax with these prayers rooted in the Scriptures, all of which end with an appeal for the Christ to 'come'. While perhaps not suitable as table prayers with very young children, they could easily and profitably be used where family members are more mature. Naturally they would need some explanation, particularly when first introduced.

O Wisdom, you come forth
from the mouth of the Most High.
You fill the universe
and hold all things together
in a strong yet gentle manner.
O come to teach us the way of truth.

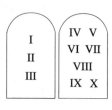

O Lord of lords and leader of Israel,
you appeared to Moses in a burning
   bush
and you gave him the Law on Sinai.
O come and save us with your mighty
   power.

O root of Jesse, you stand as a signal
   for the nations;
kings fall silent before you whom the
   peoples acclaim.
O come to deliver us, and do not delay.

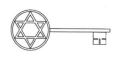

O key of David and sceptre of Israel,
what you open no one else can close
   again;
what you close no one can open.
O come to lead the captive from prison;
free those who sit in darkness and in
   the shadow of death.

O Rising Sun, you are the splendour of
   eternal light
and the sun of justice.
O come and enlighten those who sit in
   darkness
and in the shadow of death.

ADVENT

O King of the nations, whom all desire,
you are the cornerstone which makes all one.
O come and save mankind
whom you made from clay.

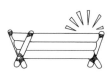

O Emmanuel, you are our king and judge,
the one whom the peoples await and their saviour.
O come and save us, Lord, our God.

Advent House

This is a similar idea to the calendar and it is made in the same way. However, unlike the calendar, it covers only the last seven days of Advent and not the whole period. The children can copy and decorate (to a uniform size) the seven symbols suggested by the antiphons, as shown above. These are positioned and glued to a piece of card or paper measuring 12 inches by 9 inches (30 cm x 22 cm). Another sheet, which is to be the top sheet of the two, and a little larger than the first one, is drawn and coloured as the front of a house with roof, door, and seven windows. Over the door, with a little decoration, can be written the words 'House of David'. The windows need to be scored down one side and cut to hinge open (just like the Advent calendar) but the actual opening is left until the appropriate day.

If you are going to use this idea it is important that the symbols are explained to the children while they are copying and colouring them. There may be a further opportunity to give a word of explanation, or encourage an older child to explain, as the windows are bent back and the symbols are revealed. Remember to explain that the 'House of David' is not literally a house.

Jesse Tree

Many parish churches have adopted this idea in recent years, and it is becoming more familiar to churchgoers. The Jesse

Tree has a longer and more Christian history than the 'traditional' Christmas tree. The Christmas tree is a well-established part of the family Christmas but it has no religious connection with the festival. It is well known that Queen Victoria's consort, Albert, brought the custom to the British Isles from Germany. It seems to have become part of Christmas there through a link with the German mystery plays of the Middle Ages. In those plays the evergreen fir tree was used to stand for the tree of good and evil in the garden of paradise.

In other parts of Europe during the Middle Ages another kind of tree was being linked with Christmas, the Jesse Tree. Although they were fairly common at that time in the stained glass window designs of many cathedrals and churches, few examples have survived. The stained glass design is based upon the Bible text:

*A shoot will come up from the stump of Jesse;
from his roots a Branch will bear fruit (Isaiah 11:1)*

(This, of course, links with the 'O' antiphons we have just talked about.) The windows show a tree, the roots being Jesse, the father of King David, then the people and events between him and Jesus are portrayed symbolically as fruit on the branches.

The ordinary family Christmas tree can be dressed up as a Jesse Tree (until Christmas Eve when it can be decorated in traditional fashion). The children may copy and then decorate cut-out pictures of symbols representing people or events that prepare the way, through the Old Testament, for the coming of Jesus. Those who use this method to make their Christmas tree fulfil a religious role in the run-up to Christmas use symbols from throughout the Old Testament and not just from King David's time onwards. For example, creation can be represented by a cut-out sun and moon; the fall of Adam and Eve by an apple. A cardboard outline of an Ark can be used for Noah and his family; a bundle of sticks for Isaac; a ladder for Jacob, a harp for King David and so on. It is certainly an excellent way for the children to become familiar with the people of the Old Testament. Bible colouring books, which can be purchased in Christian book shops around the country, can be invaluable as a basis for the decoration and the colouring.

If a family prefers not to use the Christmas tree, a small branch of a tree can be used instead. The size of the branch will depend upon whether the Jesse Tree is going to be a table decoration or stand on the floor on its own. Stripped of its bark and painted with silver paint, it can stand in a pot or suitable receptacle, awaiting the addition of the symbols, either daily from the beginning of Advent or each day of the last week.

An Advent blessing

We always think of 'blessings' as part of the work of the priest, but in fact *asking* a blessing – as distinct from *giving* a blessing – is something that anyone can do. Grace before meals is precisely that, asking God to bless the food and the meal.

If it can be arranged, a simple little ceremony asking God's blessing on the wreath, the calendar, house or tree helps to highlight the purpose of the project and set it aside as something more than a plaything. Nothing elaborate or demanding is required; simplicity is best. It should only take place when the whole family can be present. After the sign of the cross, one parent can say a prayer similar to the following:

> Heavenly Father,
> we are getting ready now
> to celebrate the coming of your Son among us.
> We ask you to bless this wreath (calendar/house)
> that we have made (decorated)
> to help us prepare well for Christmas.
> Bless too our family and all those we love.
> We ask you this through Jesus, your Son. Amen.

Conclude the little ceremony by saying the Lord's Prayer together, and/or the Hail Mary. If the calendar or house is involved then this is a good moment to open the first window.

ST NICHOLAS' DAY, 6 DECEMBER

Introductory thoughts

Some Christian families have a problem about Santa Claus or Father Christmas. They feel there is a conflict between the real meaning of Christmas and the Father Christmas myth. This should not be a problem for Catholic families with a traditional reverence for the saints of God. 'Santa Claus' is a name which has been broken down through regular use from 'Sinter Claes', which is the Dutch name for Saint Nicholas. It has entered the English language through the Dutch settlers who emigrated to North America.

Saint Nicholas lived around the fourth century and was probably the Bishop of Myra (a town which would nowadays be in modern Turkey). His existence is only known through traditional stories. It seems that after being born in Turkey he travelled widely and suffered imprisonment for his faith under the Emperor Diocletian. He was famous – so tradition has it – for his loving concern for the needy, especially children and young people.

There are many legends that tell of his generosity, but the best known concerns three marriageable young girls who could not marry because their parents were too poor to provide them with a dowry. Hearing of their plight, one night Bishop Nicholas secretly left a bag of gold at their house for the eldest daughter. Not long afterwards she found a husband. Later Nicholas crept by a second time and dropped another bag of gold through the window. The second daughter soon married. As he was about to deliver the third gift the father caught sight of him. The traditional story closes with the grateful father throwing himself at Saint Nicholas' feet, thanking him for his generosity.

Obviously this story is the basis of the Santa Claus tradition which made its way into our Christmas from the New Amsterdam (New York) Dutch who developed the traditional story into the form we now have it.

Practical suggestions

A St Nicholas service

The parish, school and family can come together to celebrate the feast of St Nicholas in such a way that the Santa Claus connection with Christmas is properly explained. In one parish, for example, each year at a suitable time on 6 December there is a special Mass for the children. A local artist has made two life-size figures, one of Saint Nicholas in his bishop's robes and the other of Father Christmas in his traditional attire. (This could equally be a project for the school.) Attention is drawn to the similarity between the white-trimmed red tunic of Santa and the episcopal robes of the Saint-Bishop. After the reading of the Gospel the celebrant recounts the story of the three young ladies and the bags of gold. The priest then calls the children up to receive a gift of a little bag of gold foil-covered chocolate coins, with a little word to each along the lines of, 'Show your love in always sharing what you have'.

If it is not possible for such a service to be held either in the parish church or the school, it can form part of the family preparations for Christmas. The parents or parent can gather the children together and tell the story, afterwards presenting the little bags of 'coins' with suitable words.

Toy service

Just as the school nativity play provides an opportunity for the home, parish and school to come together, they may also combine for an annual toy service, which involves caring for the wider neighbourhood. It is good for the children to think of Christmas as a time for giving – when God so loved us that he gave his Son. A parish (or school) toy service helps to emphasise this aspect of Christmas.

To relieve the penitential theme running throughout Advent, the Church allocates to one of the four Sundays of Advent the theme of joy – the deep peace and joy that the imminent coming of our Saviour brings us. The parish's principal Mass on the third Sunday of Advent is a very suitable time for the toy service. Parish and school can co-operate in the preparations to ensure the children are fully involved in the service, the older ones reading the intercessory prayers and the Scripture readings, the music perhaps including the school choir. The school can also support the parish effort by reminding the children to bring a toy – not a broken cast-off but a new or good-as-new one. The emphasis, it must be remembered, is not upon the toys being given, but upon the needy children of the neighbourhood who will benefit from receiving them.

After the Gospel and the priest's homily, the children can bring up their gifts as the first part of the offertory procession, and the priest can accept these before the altar. The altar servers may stack them round the base of the altar or on the altar steps, as the priest directs. If possible, a representative from the local social services can be invited to attend and offered the opportunity, at the end of the service, to accept the toys and thank the children on behalf of the needy local families.

Chapter 2
CHRISTMAS AND EPIPHANY — The Showing of Love

CHRISTMAS
Introductory thoughts

The three simple words 'I love you' are probably responsible for more joy and sorrow than any other expression. These words can be sincerely spoken and mean quite literally what they say or they can be a way to 'use' another person for extreme selfishness. We all know that it is not enough for a husband or wife to say, 'I love you'; they must show it, not just on a grand 'with-flowers' occasion, but daily in little actions of help and support. We have already spoken of giving time to our children as a genuine token of our love. Giving time to God too is an indication of our desire to return his love. Giving time to another person is the most valuable expression of love because it is a giving of ourselves and of what is most precious to us.

The Bible says, 'Yes, God loved the world so much that he gave us his only Son' (John 3:16). The Father's love for us was so great that he gave that which was most precious to him; he sent his Son into our time-world.

The arrival of a new baby

The birth of a new baby is an exciting time in a family. With understandable pride the parents show off the sign of their love for one another to family, friends and neighbours who flock to the hospital or home with useful gifts of baby clothes and accessories.

The arrival of a first baby is extra special. The genuine delight and expressions of love from everyone around the couple make the occasion unique in all human experience. Suddenly the pregnancy period, which seems so drawn out and is never without a little anxiety, is over – there is new life and much joy.

Christmas is surely the most popular of the Christian festivals because it is a celebration of 'love'. It intimately touches a deep human need. However much glitter, commercialism and hype surrounds the festival, deep down it is all about love.

At the divine level, God shows his love by giving his Son. At the human level, a young couple's first baby is born and, having no family close by, they show off their child, first to shepherds and then to the Magi (or Kings). (Luke and Matthew, in their versions of the story, point to the future role of the baby through these 'showings' – for he was to become the Good Shepherd and the King of kings.)

Everything to do with the Christian festival of Christmas is about showing love, and not, as the secular and commercial world would have us believe, simply a season for having a good time. The crib in the home, school and church shows off a baby – the sign of God's love. The cards we send, the gifts we give, show our love for one another. (We need to encourage our children to give cards not only to their friends at school, but also to those who are lonely, isolated and have few friends. We should not give in order to receive.)

Even the Christmas tree and decorations show our joy that God so loved the world that he gave us his most precious gift.

Practical suggestions
Christmas decorations

Young children love drawing, colouring and cutting out. Advent and the preparations for Christmas provide a wonderful opportunity to use their talents and enthusiasm. Individual cards that are lovingly made, no matter how simple or lacking in artistic merit, are much more in keeping with the real spirit of the festival than mass-market, shop-bought cards. (Some primary and secondary schools follow this policy and only send to governors, local authorities, suppliers, etc., cards which have been made by their pupils.) What does it matter if they are not as shiny and glittery as those everyone else has? They are more likely to be noticed, remarked upon and seen as genuine expressions of love. If such are received they should be given pride of place.

There is an obvious tension between the consumer Christmas, the secular pagan event of Christmas and the Christmas of the Church, the celebration of the Incarnation. The first seems to begin earlier every year – about the third or fourth week of October. It finishes as the shops close on 24 December. The Christian celebration begins on the evening of 24 December and extends to 6 January.

The secular Christmas puts a great deal of pressure on Christian families to conform, to anticipate the celebrations. For instance, our neighbours' homes are brightly decorated from the first week or two of December, and the children begin a bombardment of 'It's not fair, why can't we have our decorations up yet?' These entreaties should be resisted until the last possible moment, although it may not be possible to hang on until Christmas Eve! (The reason given to the children is that we cannot be waiting, in the 'coming' season, and at the same time rejoicing and celebrating Christ's arrival! Only when he is imminently due can we put up the decorations to welcome his arrival!) When Advent ends, then we pour ourselves into the celebration. But to anticipate the occasion too much and too soon is to spoil it.

To maintain peace in the family, you may want to put the decorations up gradually over a period of days, perhaps during the last week; leaving the crib until last.

Some parents may be afraid that they are being spoilsports. Why not let the children have the tree and decorations when they want them? Christmas is for children, after all. Wrong! The key-note of the 'coming' period before Christmas is the *waiting* involved in the long years before the Saviour's birth, the air of expectancy that built up as the Jews waited for their Messiah to come and deliver them. As we use an Advent calendar and wreath and pray that Christ may come, an atmosphere of expectancy is being built up in the family. This can so easily be destroyed or rendered meaningless if tree, decorations, crib and so on announce the celebration has come, when we are still in the 'coming' period.

The Christmas crib

Every family has its own way of arranging their crib. If possible it should be given a very prominent position where visitors to the family will see and benefit from it. St Francis of Assisi's original crib used living animals and real people. It was intended to teach; so should ours. It should not be treated as just another feature of the decorations, or put up idly, with little care and thought, in the way it has always been erected. Try making the children responsible for it, finding real straw to put in it, drawing and colouring a new background, arranging the figures, and so on.

Ideally the crib should not be put up until Christmas Eve or at least a couple of days before Christmas. It is a nice idea not to add the figure of the baby until just before or just after midnight Mass, or the Christmas Mass which the family attends. Some families make a little ceremony out of this. The front of the prepared stable is covered, with the other figures arranged inside. The children go upstairs (or wherever they have kept the 'baby' ready for this occasion) and bring it into the room singing *Away in a Manger* or any carol of their choice. If there are responsible older children available, they might lead a little procession with one or two lighted candles. (These could be borrowed, for the occasion, from the Advent Wreath.) When the family is gathered round the crib, the head of the family might read the following:

> 'Bless, Almighty Father, this crib which we have (made) prepared to remind us of the birth, long ago, of your beloved Son. His coming brought light and hope to the world. May our lives be lit up with our love of Jesus, who lives in our hearts by faith.

It is very important that the figures of the Magi (the three Kings) are not put in or near the crib yet. They will be added later, on the feast of the Epiphany.

Christmas gifts

The name 'Christmas' comes from the old English words *Cristes Maesse* or 'Christ's Mass', emphasising what has always been the highlight of the festival for the Catholic family. Mass together as a family, whether this is at midnight or on Christmas morning, is the special occasion we have been building up to during the weeks of Advent. (In recent years many parishes have introduced an evening Children's Mass on Christmas Eve, which is very popular and leaves the traditional Midnight Mass to the adults.) In and through the Eucharist each family group forming the parish family unites in offering the Father the gift of love that he cannot refuse. In return he gives us, in Holy Communion, our Christmas gift – His Son – as our spiritual nourishment and strength.

Each family has its own tradition of how and when to exchange Christmas gifts. Ideally this should be linked in some way with the gift we receive from God the Father. *The Christian moment*, on the day we recall how God so loved the world that he gave us his Son, is when we receive the sacramental gift of Jesus. All else, afterwards, merely celebrates this. And the first thing we can do to celebrate, if possible, is to exchange our personal gifts: our signs of love.

Celebrating a birthday

One of the first songs a toddler learns is *Happy Birthday to You*. As this comes so naturally to them, they can be encouraged to sing it on Christmas Day around the crib. It lays the foundation for a more adult understanding later on.

Excitement permitting, it may be possible to discuss with older children and teenagers what we are doing when we celebrate a birthday. They can easily grasp that a birthday celebrates the gift of life, given on a precise day at a particular moment in time. It is not the day of the year that we are celebrating, but the gift of life itself. This is obvious when we think about parents' birthdays. Most children are not very sure how old their mother or father is, and very few would know on what day of the week or at what time of the day their mother or father was born. So a birthday card and present have nothing to do with the *day* or the *time* of the birth; rather it says, 'We love you and we are grateful for your being here'. It is a celebration of life. That is why, of course, we do not celebrate the birthdays of dead members of our families.

When we celebrate the birthday of Jesus each year, we are not interested in the time of day, or the day of the week, or the year (which no one knows for certain) of his birth. We are rejoicing that Jesus, the Son of God, was born as one of us and is still alive and with us. The 'once-upon-a-time' of the inhabited crib (the first cave) only has any meaning through our faith in the empty tomb (the second cave). If we did not believe that Christ was now alive and with us, there would never have been any such event as Christmas. This is why Easter is more important than Christmas.

The twelve days of Christmas

For the Christian family, Christmas continues until 6 January. Although parents may return to work and the children may even return to school, the Christmas season is not closed until after the celebration of the Epiphany. So the decorations should not come down until the Wise Men (or if you prefer, the three kings) have had a chance to get to the crib! Everyone would agree that these three traditional figures play an important part in the Christmas scenario, but so often they play little or no part in the celebrations.

In the early centuries of the Church, when Christ's birthday was celebrated (it was not for the first 250 years), it was observed by the Eastern Christians on 6 January and by the Western Christians on 25 December. Of course this caused some confusion! It was resolved in the end by the Western Church extending their celebrations to 6 January which became the feast of 'the showing' or manifestation, which is the meaning of the word 'Epiphany'. So we now have the famous 'twelve days of Christmas', from 25 December to 6 January.

Feast of the family

> 'Last year we went to your parents on Christmas Day and my family on Boxing Day . . . I think we ought to visit my parents this Christmas; we can go to your folks on Boxing Day'
>
> 'No, that won't work, if we do that we'll . . .

Every year many families face the problem of who is going where and when over Christmas. A great effort is made to get together and not miss anyone out over the holiday period. To be together, to show our love for each other over those three or four days in the year, is what really matters. No matter how much has been spent on Christmas gifts, it is the giving, in person if possible, which counts. Love is best expressed in giving. It is at this time that the description of the family by Pope John Paul II, as 'the community of love' is most evident.

The Church very wisely takes advantage of all this by emphasising the importance and value of the family. It places the feast of the Holy Family on 30 December. The point of this is not just to remind us that the individual members of that family were all 'holy', but that the way to holiness for the great majority of us is through the family. 'Christian marriage is the pathway to holiness for all members of the family' (Pope John Paul II).

We have to help our children (and ourselves too, for that matter) to an understanding that 'holiness' does not mean 'odd', 'peculiar' or 'abnormal'. For this reason, the family of Nazareth were seen by their neighbours to be quite ordinary and normal, doing all the usual things that families do. Most pictures of the Holy Family are unhelpful and to be avoided! At best they are sentimental and at worst they are so misleading as to present, in the long term, possible danger to the child's faith.

A word or two of explanation: certainly we believe that Jesus is, and will always be, the Son of God. But that belief cannot be allowed to under-value, or perhaps even destroy, our like belief that he was a normal human being as well: like us in *all* things, Paul reminded us, except that he could not sin. Little boys can do lots of naughty things that are not 'sins'. Untidiness is not a sin, a dirty face is not sinful, and so on. If in later life the man Jesus was so obviously normal and ordinary-looking that his closest friends took a long time, and indeed found it difficult to say, 'You are the Messiah', he must have looked and behaved very like any other village lad in Nazareth. So the Holy Family was just like ours – with only one difference – there was no deliberate offence given to God. That leaves plenty of room for Mary and Joseph to struggle with their impatience when Jesus was naughty; for Mary and Joseph to have different views and opinions about how Jesus should be brought up; for Joseph to be worried sick about where his next job or piece of work was coming from; for Mary to be subjected to the latest piece of hot gossip over the garden wall! That the boy Jesus could cause worry can be seen from the only glimpse we get of life in the Holy Family (in Luke's Gospel) when, at the age of 12, he was lost in Jerusalem.

The best way to note this feast day in the family, besides a special grace at meal times (see page 57) is to discuss and bring out the humanness of this special family. Mothers, in their own personal prayers, can and should ask Mary, as an understanding mother, to help the family with her prayers. Fathers too should not hesitate to ask Joseph for some assistance when housing causes headaches, money is scarce, or unemployment threatens.

EPIPHANY – THE SHOWING
Introductory thoughts

Surprisingly the feast of the Epiphany is older than Christmas itself, being kept in the Eastern part of the Roman Empire from the very earliest times. It still remains a more important day than 25 December for most Eastern Christians. This is probably because they have retained a better understanding of what the feast means than we have. Epiphany is the showing of the infant Jesus to the non-Jewish Magi, emphasising that the Christian Faith is to be for all, not just for the Jews.

Practical suggestions

There are a few simple ceremonies that can help the family to mark this special day. The Magi, or kings, were not put into the crib (see page 30) on Christmas Eve. Some families have the lovely little custom of making them travel to the crib from a starting point somewhere in the house. The starting point of the figures need not be in the same room; instead of arid deserts, mountain ranges and rivers, the figures can be assisted, day after day, across carpets, furniture and stairs. They can set out on Christmas Eve and after the hazards of the journey arrive outside the crib on 6 January. With the aid of a strip of adhesive tape, a star can travel a little ahead of them. The shepherds, of course, will have been removed long before the Magi arrive, to make room for them, so that it is clearly their special day.

Dressing up

Young children, especially girls, love dressing up and this is the ideal feast day for that. The event is tailor-made for dressing up and playing out the story. It is important to remember that although *tradition* says there were *three* wise men or kings, the Gospel of Matthew (which is the only one to tell the story) does not say how many there were. It merely says 'some wise men came from the East' (Matthew 2:1). Now this is very useful to remember if there are insufficient children for three 'kings'. (Show the children the text if you can.) If there are more than three children, they can all be 'kings', and naturally these 'kings' will need attendants, not to mention camels and donkeys!

Making crowns and gifts and dressing up can take the best part of an afternoon. Either the gifts could be especially made for the occasion or household items, such as jewellery cases or music boxes, could be commandeered (with permission). The 'journey' or procession from a bedroom to the crib can be made into a splendid affair. After the presentation of the gifts at the crib, have a little surprise party (Mum or Dad can prepare this secretly while all the dressing up, etc., is taking place; it will make the occasion a special treat and all the more memorable). Make a simple 'crown' cake, or sponge cake baked in the rough shape of a crown and encrusted with small colourful sweets representing jewels. Presented after the 'gold', 'frankincense' and 'myrrh', the little party will not only round off the celebration perfectly but will also help the children to appreciate that Christian festivals can be fun.

Epiphany blessing
Since very early times tradition has had it that there were three visitors to the child Jesus. This tradition probably arose because three gifts were given. The visitors were usually thought of as kings, possibly because of Psalm 72, which says, 'The kings of Tarshish and of the islands will pay him tribute. The kings of Sheba and Seba will offer gifts.' At some time in the remote and distant past they were given the names of Caspar, Melchior and Baltassar (or Balthasar).

In some countries, where the greater number of the population is Catholic, for example in Poland, there is a very ancient tradition of a special blessing for the home at Epiphany time. The blessing is closely associated with Caspar, Melchior and Baltassar. After the blessing of the home, the family chalks up the following sign, C + M + B + (the year) over the doorway. If it is not possible for a priest to come and bless the house, the head of the household could ask a blessing on the home.

THE BAPTISM OF JESUS
Introductory thoughts
After thinking about babies and families for so long it comes as something of a shock on the very first Sunday after the Epiphany to find the Church wanting us to consider the Baptism of Jesus at the age of thirty! Naturally, being a Jewish little boy, Jesus was named at his circumcision, a few days after his birth. It is his public work as a preacher that begins with his baptism by his cousin John. His circumcision was a quiet family affair involving only his immediate family, but

his baptism, when he took up his preaching work, was a very public act – a showing to the world: another epiphany or manifestation.

When we thought about the 'coming' season before Christmas, we discovered that the Church wants us to realise that there are three 'comings' of Christ. At Christmas time too we are helped to see that there was more than one 'showing' of Jesus. As a new born baby he was shown first to the shepherds (he would become the Good Shepherd); some time later he was shown to the Magi, or kings (he would be the 'King of kings'); and now, as a man, he is marked out among the crowds.

You will remember what happened: Jesus, trying to find out what his Father wanted him to do, went up from his home in Nazareth to the place on the banks of the Jordan where his cousin John was preaching and baptising. There Jesus asked to be baptised and as he came up out of the water a voice spoke from heaven: 'This is my Son, the Beloved; my favour rests on him' (Matthew 3:17, NJB).

Jesus, of course would have been 'ducked under' by John in the waters of the Jordan. This was the method of the early Church; in some places, in the Catholic Church, it is being reintroduced.

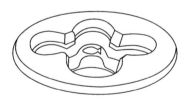

This picture shows a kind of font or baptistery that was used by the Church in the first two or three hundred years of its existence. This drawing is based upon a font preserved in a museum in Carthage, North Africa.

It was used in this way: the adult wanting to join the Christian community showed her/his faith and love for Christ by passing through the waters of baptism to a new life.

The priest would stand at point P, the catechumen (the adult convert) at point C and a deacon at point D. After making an act of faith, the catechumen would step down into the water in the centre (it was probably lapping over their feet where they were standing at C). The priest would help the convert to submerge in the water while he, the priest, said the words of the sacrament: 'I baptise you in the name of the Father and of the Son and of the Holy Spirit.' As the new Christian emerged from the water the deacon would wrap a white baptismal robe round them.

The convert may well have been presented at the same time with a lighted candle, a symbol of their new role as light-bearer, to follow Christ, 'the light of the world', and take Christ's light out to the world. With this method of baptising, the new Christian passed *through* the waters of baptism as well as going *under* the waters. This was also achieved by and through the cross. It was in this way that the early Church kept Paul's words in mind: 'We were therefore buried with him through baptism into death in order that, just as Christ was raised from the dead through the glory of the Father, we too may live a new life' (Romans 6:4).

At that time the acceptance of baptism was a very solemn and life-changing act. It was the most dramatic and important step that a person would ever take. The complete commitment and gift of self to Christ could, and in thousands of cases did, result in torture and death. (Yet so many people accepted the challenge of baptism that within three hundred years the work of that little band of twelve apostles had resulted in the virtual conversion of the Roman world.) Those who escaped martyrdom must have lived out their lives of commitment and been real 'lights' to the world.

However hard we, today, try to make the baptism of a baby full of meaning and purpose, it lacks the dramatic impact originally experienced. Most of us were baptised as children and of course have not the faintest memory of the most important religious act in our life. That is why parents must not lightly ask for baptism for their child and must look for every possible means to prepare themselves and the godparents well for the sacrament.

In recent years a great effort has been made in most parishes to help adult Catholics come to a better knowledge and appreciation of their faith. This usually takes the form of an occasional course or series of talks. Faced with children's needs and questioning, parents will realise their own need for a more mature grasp of the Faith. Opportunities to put this right should be seized and used.

Practical suggestions

Because at baptism parents act on behalf of their child in saying, 'This is what we ask for our child', they must, as the child grows up, help them to understand what has happened. In practice this means, among other things, not missing an opportunity to recall and celebrate the anniversary of the child's baptism. The feast of Christ's baptism is one such opportunity when the child's baptismal candle can be got out and used as a table centrepiece, lit for a few minutes at the Sunday meal with a word or two of explanation.

Gifts that a child receives on his or her christening day usually disappear into cupboards or drawers. As a continual reminder of that important day (assuming that the gifts are suitable) a special shelf, part of a bookcase or similar could be set aside for the gifts to be displayed. The baptismal candle and certificate should be given pride of place. Such a display is a continual reminder to the whole family of the importance of baptism.

Christmas is a time for the family. It is the time when we recall the Holy Family and immediately afterwards we are reminded that as Christians we are adopted members of God's family – sons and daughters of God through our baptism.

Showing love to other members of the Christian family

It cannot be a coincidence that the week of Prayer for Christian Unity follows so soon after Christmas, from 18 January to 25 January. This week should not pass by unnoticed.

As family life is the setting in which children grow to understand and share love, it is there too that they learn what unity is. There is no better place for an understanding love of other Christians to grow and be nurtured.

Some families, of course, are members of more than one denomination; but many more consist of a Catholic and a partner who is not committed to any particular Church. In both cases the family has an opportunity to talk and pray about Church differences. Of course there has to be a lot of sensitivity on the Catholic partner's side, to avoid making a non-Catholic partner feel 'got at' or 'put on the spot'. Nor should impertinent questions be tolerated from younger members of the family; at all times an individual's freedom of choice and personal decision should be respected. It should be made clear, in talking with young people, that adults have made their own responsible free decision.

Many parishes receive the annual prayer leaflet issued by The Churches Together in England and Wales. The family might like to acquire a copy for use in the home. It gives a list of prayer intentions for use over the eight days, and also some prayers, which may need to be adapted for use in the home. While not all of the leaflet will be helpful for family prayer, it should act as a stimulus.

Learning how to show love is the family's work and showing love to our brothers and sisters in the wider Christian family should be very high on our list of priorities.

Chapter 3
LENT AND HOLY WEEK
The Offering of Love

Introductory thoughts

Two-year-old Sharon and her friend Michael, who was nearly 4, were playing happily in the garden. Suddenly their mothers, who were enjoying a quiet cup of coffee in the kitchen, were disturbed by a great commotion. Rushing to the window they saw both children trying to jam themselves, at the same time, on the seat of the one and only tricycle. After much shouting and screeching both managed to squeeze on, but neither could move! When their mothers got to them Sharon was sobbing and Michael was stoutly and loudly proclaiming, 'If one of us got off *I* could ride it properly!'

It was resolved that they would take turns. Michael had the first short ride up the concrete garden path, pursued after less than thirty seconds by Sharon, calling, 'Me turn, me turn'.

Experienced parents will recognise this as an everyday sort of occurrence when young children are playing together. 'Me-me-me' is a regularly heard cry and the attitude underlying all the play of very young children. When the youngster follows their natural desire to eat with their fingers, drop food all over the floor or squat on the carpet behind the settee instead of on the potty, a parent realises how close the young human is to the animal kingdom! This closeness shows particularly in the instinctive drive for self-preservation; for example, taking handfuls of biscuits or sweets, instead of the one expected. The 'me-me-me' and the strong natural self-love it demonstrates is the self-preservation instinct in full swing.

Learning unselfish love

One of parents' most important tasks is to develop in their children an awareness and love of others – quite simply to teach them to share. This is something that has to be *learned*, just as the child has to learn how to use a knife and fork safely. No one *naturally* puts others first, before him or herself.

That natural and necessarily strong self-love that we are each born with has to be broadened out, channelled and developed. While retaining a healthy self-love (so that we look after ourselves properly and avoid danger), in-growing love has to be turned out to others. The child learns to share by the way the family life is organised and run. They learn principally by example. In play too the child learns to take turns with others.

The learning goes on all through life. There is no cut-off point because we are all, to a greater or lesser degree, selfish people. The really mature person is the one who is most unselfish, who has the greatest love and consideration for others. Our daily newspapers sometimes carry stories of heroic unselfishness:

'Wife throws herself in front of husband as terrorist fires.'
'Scout leader shields youngster from falling rocks with his own body.'

Other people live heroically unselfish lives hardly noticed by the world, as, patiently and lovingly, year in and year out, they care for a very demanding physically or mentally handicapped child.

Jesus summed all this up when he said, 'Greater love has no one than this, that he lay down his life for his friends' (John 15:13).

Love compels action; the wife did not stop to think – should she or should she not shield her husband? – nor did the scout leader. A 'me-me-me' person would not have acted! Only years of generous self-giving could prompt such an immediate offering of oneself.

Growth to maturity

True Christian maturity has nothing to do with being physically big and strong or good- or bad-looking; nothing to do with being well educated; nothing to do with being black or white or this nationality or that. True Christian maturity has everything to do with struggling daily with self-love and developing an outward-going love of others. We are reminded, yet again, of Paul's words:

> If I have all the eloquence of men or of angels, but speak without love, I am simply a gong booming or a cymbal clashing. If I have the gift of prophecy, understanding all the mysteries there are, and knowing everything, and if I have faith in all its fullness, to move mountains, but without love, then I am nothing at all' (1 Corinthians 13:1-2, author's paraphrase)

There is only one road to maturity and that is the road of self-discipline. This means working with God's grace to turn an in-growing love outwards, or more simply saying 'no' more often to ourselves and 'yes' to others.

Family life is not easy! Nor is learning self-discipline. Parents are learning self-discipline at the same time as they are teaching it to their children. In fact, the very living-out of daily family life is a discipline for parents. The good mother runs around at the beck and call of the family when she would love to sit quiet for a few minutes; the good father will play with the children and read to them before becoming engrossed in the sports page.

Children can only learn self-discipline by learning to obey in the home. Youngsters will never learn to say 'no' to themselves later in life if they have not learned to respond to the 'no' said to them in the family. An obedience based on love is all-important. This is the sort of obedience Jesus expects of his followers. 'If you love me,' he says, 'you will do what I ask' (John 15:10, author's paraphrase).

And what does he ask? 'You must love your neighbour as yourself' (Matthew 19:19). Failing to do that is to sin.

Deliberately to turn love, which should be given to 'Love' itself, in on ourselves is to offend God.

THE SEASON OF LENT

Lent is the season offered to us by the Church during which we can make a special effort with self-discipline. It is *offered* to us because we can quite easily sail through Lent without using the opportunity. But if we do that we and our family are the losers. We will receive encouragement but no one will check up to see if we respond or not.

Named after the old English word 'lenten', which means 'spring', the season was first intended as a preparation period for the new converts who were getting ready for baptism. In the early years of Christianity this took place at the Easter Vigil. Later the season was applied to all Christians and their need for an annual effort to renew themselves. Christians who had sinned seriously and now wanted to return to the active life of the community were prepared throughout these forty days for reconciliation at Easter. As a sign of their sorrow they wore clothes of sacking and ashes were sprinkled on their heads. By the ninth century this custom had stopped and was replaced by a ceremony involving the whole Church. To remind the whole community that each and every one was a sinner, ashes were placed on their heads on the first day of Lent. Since this took place on a Wednesday, the day naturally became Ash Wednesday.

TO EASTER THROUGH LENT

Only Easter makes sense of Lent. Only the resurrection makes sense of Christ's birth, life and death. Jesus' death, on its own, was not special. He offered himself to his Father on the cross, but if the Father had not accepted his offering that would have been the end of it. However, the Father did show his acceptance by raising his Son up to a new life. Easter is, for that reason, the most important festival in the Church's year, the celebration of the main event of God's work in the world.

Given the great fuss that is made of Christmas it is not surprising that most people fail to appreciate the importance of Easter. Children find it particularly difficult to take in. All those lovely presents, decorations and parties around Christmas time stand in strong contrast to what happens at Easter! A few chocolate Easter eggs do not redress the balance! In the family a great effort needs to be made to give the celebration of Easter a proper emphasis and dignity. And this is not possible without taking the forty days of Lent seriously.

What we have got to absorb and gradually impart to our family is the message of Lent. This is, as we have been saying, that we must die to our own selfishness so that we can rise up joyfully with Christ to a new life.

- It is *a time for – a change of heart.* A time for a new and closer look at the way our lives are lived, for repentance and reconciliation.
- It is *a time for – concern for others.* Caring for others is a valuable weapon in our fight against selfishness. Almsgiving has always been a part of Lent.
- It is a *time for – prayer which costs.* That means in terms of time and personal effort.

When any 'giving-up' or mortification is spoken of at the outset of Lent these three things must be kept in mind – our need for a change of heart, an outward and genuine concern for others and, underlying everything, a need to pray much more.

Each of these three parts to Lent must be present if the season is to have any real and lasting value. To go into Lent with a resolution to give up sugar in our tea, for example, is only of any value if it is part of our 'change of heart' campaign. The money saved should go to our deprived brothers and sisters and the action supported by an increased effort at prayer.

Practical suggestions
ASH WEDNESDAY

From breakfast on Ash Wednesday morning the family needs to understand that the next few weeks point us to the celebration of Christ's resurrection. Grace before meals can keep Easter in mind from the beginning.

For children actions speak louder than words, so attendance at the Mass of the Ashes is important. The simple dramatic symbolism can mark very clearly the special nature of this time. Seeing who has still got ashes visible at the evening meal time can lead naturally into some talk about the meaning of the ashes and so on to the purpose of Lent.

Family service of the ashes

If the family cannot get to a Mass at which the ashes are blessed and bestowed then a little evening ceremony in the home is easily arranged. The correct procedure is to make the ashes from the palms given the previous year on Palm Sunday. Many families keep their blessed palms but if you have not done so another piece of (dry) evergreen would do. (Always save your palms from one year to the next, just in case you need them.) If one or two members of the family have already received the ashes there is no reason why they cannot also take part in a private family celebration.

Just before or after the evening meal is a good time for this service. It could be an extended 'grace' or 'table prayer'. Cut a couple of the small individual palms up into short pieces and burn them carefully in a small basin or saucer. The head of the household can read a prayer of blessing similar to the following over them:

> Let us ask our heavenly Father to bless these ashes which we will use as a mark of our repentance (pause).
>
> Lord, bless these ashes.
> Wearing them reminds us
> that we are from the dust of the earth.

> Pardon our sins and keep us faithful
> to the resolutions we have made for Lent.
> Help us to prepare well
> for the celebrations of your Son's glorious resurrection.
> This we ask through the same Jesus Christ. Amen.

Then dipping his thumb in the ashes, he marks each forehead with the words:

> Turn away from sin and be faithful to the Gospel.

The simple ceremony can close with this prayer:

> Loving Father, today we start Lent.
> Over the next six weeks, with your help,
> we are going to prepare for Easter.
> From today we are making a new start
> with a bigger effort to be more loving and kind.
> Help us to show concern for the less fortunate,
> the hungry and the poor,
> And especially help us to speak to you more often.
> We ask this through your Son, Jesus,
> whose death and resurrection we will be thinking about
> in the next few weeks. Amen.

Younger members of the family may well get a fit of the giggles. If they do, allow it to take its course without overreacting. This is no reason for abandoning or not trying a worthwhile ceremony. Simple action signs repeated year after year have a lasting impact.

Resolutions for Lent

Faithfully and sincerely living the Christian life means a continual effort to live up to the ideals Christ has set us. Because we so regularly fall short we are constantly picking ourselves up and making a new effort, a new beginning.

Lent is a terrific opportunity to make such a fresh start. This in effect means making resolutions. They should be few, practical and reasonable. A little self-knowledge should be brought to bear. It is quite pointless making great promises, for example to go to daily Mass, if you know yourself well enough to know that you will not keep it up. However, you might reasonably organise yourself to get to Mass once or twice in the week.

Besides the above there is only one golden rule about Lenten resolutions. Never give up or take up anything that will have an adverse effect upon the family. The classic example is smoking – if Dad's resolution to give up smoking makes him like a bear with a sore head and a 'pain' to live with, he must not do it, at least not during Lent. On the other hand Dad or Mum's smoking may already be very unpleasant and unhealthy for the rest of the family. Then one might give up smoking as a mark of love and respect for those who share the same home.

Having a change of heart does not mean being miserable or making others suffer. If Mum's resolution to help with the church cleaning during Lent takes her away from her own cleaning and household duties or means the house is empty when the children come home from school then she should find something else to do.

Nothing that is done supposedly for the love of God should ever be undertaken if it interferes with our love and responsibility for the family. Our first duty is to love God through the loving service we give to our family.

Preparing for Reconciliation

Selfishness and self-love are the enemies we are out to deal a blow to during Lent. We should try to see our resolutions and Lenten efforts as a preparation for the sacrament of reconciliation (confession).

Going to confession is not something we 'fit in' in order to fulfil a duty just before Easter. Receiving the ashes at the start of Lent should be seen as the start of our six weeks of preparation for receiving the sacrament in Holy Week.

In most parishes the children of 7 and older make their first confession during this traditional period of sorrow for sin. This is a time of special co-operation between school, parish and home – the triangle of educational and pastoral care.

Local ways of proceeding vary from place to place, although most parishes now have teams of lay people who prepare the children in the setting of the parish. This, among other things, allows parents and families to be more involved than in the past. This is a most important time for the children. They did not choose to be baptised nor, of course, do they remember it. This is therefore their first voluntary public religious act. On no account should a child be forced, pressurised or bribed into receiving the sacrament – or going to Holy Communion – for the first time. There is no harm done by leaving it another year or two. What other people, including teachers and clergy, may say or think must be regarded purely as advice. The parent has the final decision. If the child is clearly not ready or is unwilling, on no account should she or he be talked into it. The dignity of the sacraments demands that they should always be received willingly. To coerce a child may well set up a chain reaction and sow the seeds of a total rejection of Christianity later on.

The willing child should be helped to see that going to the sacraments for the first time is an important step towards becoming a grown-up Christian. It is like a first sign of a 'coming of age', because now they will be bound, as are adults, to go to Mass on Sundays and Holy Days.

Fridays of Lent

The final few days of Lent are the climax of these six weeks, and the most important of these days is Good Friday, the day which casts its long shadow over the preceding weeks. All our efforts at self-discipline – saying 'no' to ourselves – are only of any real value if they are linked to Christ's love and obedience, which took him to the cross. It is his obedient love that wins for us the forgiveness of the Father. And he will bless our efforts and raise us up if all that we do in Lent is offered with and through his obedient Son.

In the Church's calendar each week is thought of as the year in miniature. The highlight of the year is Easter Sunday – the highlight of the week is Sunday, when we gather together to recall and celebrate Christ's rising from the dead.

In the same way, every Friday we are asked to recall the events of Good Friday.

Fish on Fridays

The 'why' of the old rule about 'fish on Fridays' (really it was abstaining from meat) is not often explained. It became just one of those odd things that Catholics did. The original intention was that each Friday we should recall that this was the day of the week on which Jesus died, and in recalling this that we would mark it with an act of sorrow for sin.

When the obligation to abstain from meat on a Friday was done away with (not a lot of point when two-thirds of the world *never* see meat to eat) we were asked to carry on doing something of our own choosing. The day still needed to be marked out as we always need to express sorrow for sin. Sadly, very few people ever think about it!

The six (seven including Good Friday) Fridays of Lent are a little special and – together with Sundays – can be the focal points of the weeks of Lent. One way to use the day is to link the ancient tradition of fasting during Lent with the concern we should have for the deprived. CAFOD (Catholic Fund for Overseas Development) organises one special 'family fast day' in Lent, but there is no good reason why families cannot make every Friday a 'family fast day'. By going without one full meal or reducing two of the meals, and donating to charity the money we would have spent on feeding ourselves, our own 'no' to ourselves can be a positive 'yes' to the needy.

Friday prayer

The 'table prayer' of Lenten Fridays also offers an opportunity to make these days a bit different. At the principal meal of the day when hopefully most of the family is present, an adapted and simplified Way of the Cross can be used. There are two methods of using it. The first way, in a family where the children are quite young, is to spread the seven 'stations' over the seven Fridays of Lent, one each week. The second method, where the family is older, is to use the whole thing each week (or selected parts: for example the 'stations' that can be found in the Gospels) involving if possible each member of the family round the table. You will need to bring your Bible to the table.

Way of the Cross

This is set out here for use week by week over a period of seven weeks. If it is all to be used at one time, ignore the references to 'First Friday', 'Second Friday' and so on.

First Friday of Lent

1. *Jesus is condemned to death*
Read John 19:4-11 and 16.
Let us say sorry to God for the times we have talked unkindly and unjustly about other people (and called them names).
Please, God, help us not to judge others. Amen.

Second Friday of Lent

2. *Jesus is met by his mother*
Tradition tells us that Jesus met Mary on the Way of the Cross. Certainly Mary's great love would have prompted her to be there. This love-poem from the Bible tells us how she would have felt: 'I will rise now and go about the city, in the streets and in the squares; I will seek him whom my soul loves' (Song of Songs 3:1-4).
Let us say we are sorry to God for the times we have upset and hurt those we love most.
Please, God, help us to love and respect our family. Amen.

Third Friday of Lent

3. *The cross is laid upon Simon of Cyrene*
Read Mark 15:21.
Let us tell God that we are sorry for the times when we have not offered to help other people, especially people in real need.
Please, God, help us to give our help generously
to anyone who needs it. Amen.

Fourth Friday of Lent
4. *The women of Jerusalem mourn for Our Lord*
   Read Luke 23:27-32.
   Let us say sorry to God for the times when we have been proud and not admitted that we were in the wrong.
   Please, God, help us to be humble
   and ask forgiveness when we have sinned. Amen.

Fifth Friday of Lent
5. *Jesus is stripped of his clothes*
   Read John 19:23-24.
   Let us tell God how sorry we are for the times when we have been selfish and pushed ourselves in front of others.
   Please, God, help us to strip ourselves of our selfishness. Amen.

Sixth Friday of Lent
6. *Jesus is nailed to the cross*
   Read Luke 23:33-34.
   Let us say sorry to God for the times when our hands and feet have led us into sin.
   Please, God, help us to be always honest and trustworthy. Amen.

Seventh Friday of Lent
7. *Jesus dies on the cross*
   Read Matthew 27:45-50.
   Let us say sorry to God for all the times we have failed in our love for him and not obeyed his wishes.
   Please, God, help us to grow in love for you
   and give you the obedience you look for. Amen.

The Easter tree
We are very fortunate that in our part of the world the seasonal pattern of nature helps us to a better understanding

of the meaning of Lent and Easter. The apparently dead winter trees and bushes are gradually transformed during this period. By Easter Sunday fresh green leaves are showing the rebirth of nature. What was dead, dark and cold is showing life, light and hope. As far as possible, according to where you live, the children's attention needs to be drawn to this annual transformation in nature. Of course, a parallel should be drawn with our own lives as Christians.

The Easter tree is one good way of tying the two together. On a large sheet of white card, or poster board, or perhaps on a surface taken from the inside of a large (empty) cereal packet, draw a simple outline of a tree in winter, including the roots. Cut out the outline (don't make the branches and twigs too detailed otherwise there will be problems) leaving the roots in the ground. Get the children to colour the trunk and branches brown – nothing more, because it is representing an apparently dead tree in winter. Mount the tree on a second piece of board, allowing about a quarter of an inch (or a centimetre) between the two cards. Write the heading 'Easter Tree' above the tree on the backing card. On Ash Wednesday hang the Easter Tree in your kitchen where everyone can see it. On that day get the children to fill a sheet (possibly one each) with little ovals which they colour green. These are to be the leaves and their dimension should be kept in some sort of proportion with the tree.

The tree works alongside the resolutions that have been made by the family for Lent (see page 47). Each time (perhaps once a day so that they can all be done together) a good turn has been done, or a resolution kept, a green leaf is stuck onto the tree. By the time Easter Sunday comes the tree should be covered in foliage. The roots, which should not have been coloured brown when the trunk was, can be coloured in for each of the Sunday Masses and holy communions of Lent: it is from our Sunday worship together and the reception of the risen Christ in holy communion, that the grace and strength comes to live our lives as children of God. It is from union with Christ and his community that we receive the grace and strength to do good.

On Easter Day the tree will serve as a decoration and lovely memorial of our efforts throughout Lent. On Easter morning, to symbolise the resurrection, little yellow or white bows can be tied between the green leaves around the branches.

MOTHER'S DAY

The Fourth Sunday of Lent, which is also called *Laetare Sunday*, is traditionally known as 'Mothering Sunday' or, in our secular world of today, 'Mother's Day'. In modern times, probably due more to the influence of the large greetings card companies than the Christian Church, it is one of the most popular celebrations of the year. It is of interest to note that it often falls close to 25 March, nine months prior to Christmas Day, when the Virgin Mary was invited to be the mother of the Lord.

For centuries before the Reformation, devout parishioners used to go to the mother church of their diocese, the cathedral, to make special offerings on this Sunday. Exactly when the day also became a festival of human motherhood is uncertain, but 'going a-mothering', that is, visiting your mother with a gift, was well established in Britain by the seventeenth century. Apprentices and servants were given the day off to take a cake or a posy of primroses or violets, gathered in the hedgerows on the way, as a gift to their mothers.

All families develop their own way of celebrating this day; all that needs to be added is to remember a special prayer of thanksgiving, especially as part of the grace that day, for the mothers, including the grandmothers, of the whole extended family.

HOLY WEEK

The three very special days of the week we call 'holy' – Thursday, Friday and Sunday – are the pinnacle of the Church's year. Everything else in the year either builds up to these three days or looks back to them. They are rather like the Holy Trinity – three but one: three days making up one event – the 'passover' of Jesus. Parents really need to read and think about all this in order to be able to help their children understand and join fully in the celebration of Easter.

The meaning of the Easter candle, our Easter tree, even Easter eggs, will be lost if the three days are not explained and celebrated as *one* event.

The three days actually are:

Maundy Thursday evening to Good Friday evening	Last Supper and death of Jesus
Good Friday evening to Saturday evening	Burial and 'silence' of grave
Saturday evening to Easter Sunday evening	Resurrection

- Jesus offers himself
- The offering is accepted
- The offering (Jesus) is given back to us

(The Church has always followed the Jewish custom of starting the day not at sunrise but at sunset on the day before. This allows us to go to Mass on Saturday evening and still fulfil the Sunday Mass obligation. Saturday evening is really the beginning of Sunday.)

PRAYER IN THE FAMILY

Introductory thoughts

This section is included here because a lot of parents would like their family to pray together but, not knowing how to get started or feeling too embarrassed to suggest it, never get round to it. The beginning of Lent provides the perfect opportunity to make a start. And making a resolute start is half the battle; the other half consists in trying to remember to do it every day, keeping it simple and trying to make it enjoyable. Before we look at each of those points in turn there are a few background thoughts to keep in mind.

Background

'Ann looks more like her mother every day.'

'Richard loves sport like his dad.'

Inevitably our children grow up looking a bit like us, with some of our mannerisms, habits and interests. It is sure to happen because from their very earliest moments they have watched us closely and have imitated us.

When we start talking about prayer we must not forget that prayer cannot be *taught*, it has to be *caught*. If Mum and Dad do not see the real point of praying and only 'go through the motions', then children will sense this immediately. It is a total waste of time for parents to send young children off to bed with a 'Don't forget your prayers', then turn their attention straight back to their favourite television programme. Children will only learn to pray if they see their parents praying.

The first point to make, then, is that if you want your family to pray *you* must pray yourself and allow your children to see you pray. This is sure to mean sacrificing yourself a little – not sinking into the newspaper so quickly in the evening, for instance, or perhaps missing some viewing time.

From the beginning it is a good idea for the parents to keep the target or goal in mind: to get the family – over a period of time – so 'at home' with prayer that it becomes natural for them to pray easily anywhere, at any time, about any- and everything.

A resolute start

The younger the children, the easier it is to start. Most teenagers get embarrassed about praying with the family (they are frightened their friends will find out and they will be made to look silly in front of them) but this should not stand in the way of the rest of the family going ahead. Many a conscientious objector secretly wants to take part in spite of her/himself and later will find it possible to join in. No child is too young to be included and often it is the youngest who will remind the others that it is time to talk to God!

Having made up your mind, fix a definite starting time; for example the evening meal of Ash Wednesday when all the family might be together. There is no better way to start than with grace before meals. This wonderful old custom has largely fallen into disuse, in part because meals have become, in so many families, fragmented things. For example: Paul is eating now, because he has to rush off to football practice; Clare eats a little later because she could not be enticed away from the TV any sooner; Dad a bit later still, because his train was late getting in, and so on.

Mealtimes should be focal points of the day, when the family (or as much of it as possible) is together, sharing the same table, the same food and the conversation. Every effort should be made to keep the family united in this (see page 77); there is a lot more at stake – in the long term – than a football practice, or a TV story. So often one hears of a family that has fallen apart because the various members have not communicated with one another. They have each gone their own way, strangers to one another in the same building. As soon as the first child can sit in a high chair the family tradition of always eating together – unless really impossible – should be established.

Grace before meals is a good place to start family prayer because it is generally a recognised and understood prayer with which people are familiar. Use a simple prayer to begin with, perhaps the traditional one: 'Bless us, O Lord, and these thy gifts which we are about to receive from thy bounty', or one of the following short prayers, or possibly one the children use at school. This will get over the natural awkwardness of a new experience.

> Come, Lord Jesus, be our guest,
> and may our meal by you be blest. Amen.

> Great God and giver of all good,
> accept our praise and bless our food.
> Grace, health and strength to us afford
> through Jesus Christ, our risen Lord. Amen.
> (Jeremiah Clarke)

Lord Jesus, be our guest,
our morning prayer,
our evening rest,
and with this daily food, impart
your love and grace to every heart. Amen.

Be present at our table, Lord,
be here and everywhere adored. Amen.

All good gifts around us
are sent from heaven above.
Then thank the Lord, O thank the Lord,
for all his love. Amen.

Take care not to get stuck on the same grace; variety will keep it more interesting. After using a set formula or pattern of words for your daily grace before meals for a little while, try making up your own. (Say grace after meals too if you can manage it, although this is not quite so important and may be difficult to keep going with younger members of the family leaving the table before the adults.) Your own prayer can be very short and simple and begin with, 'Please, Father, bless us and the food we are about to eat'. Later it can grow a little to express thanks for good health and family unity and prayer for the hungry of the world.

Holding hands round the table while grace is being said is very popular with the younger children. It is also symbolic of family unity and easily leads into prayers like: 'Bless our family circle, Lord, and keep us united in your love. May we always be grateful for the food we eat and for all the good things we receive from your hand.'

Table prayers

These are really no more than a longer form of grace. On notable occasions, when something special is called for (for example, Christmas, Ash Wednesday, Fridays of Lent), rather than call the family together at a different and perhaps artificial time for prayers to mark the occasion, it is better to extend the grace at the evening meal or main meal of the day.

LENT AND HOLY WEEK

Night prayers

The custom of praying privately last thing at night continues in many Catholic families. It can be made into one of the two focal points around which family prayer develops.

Parents cannot start night prayers too early with young children. (Not, of course, merely to listen to the child reciting their prayers, but to say little impromptu prayers with and for the child.) Such prayers can begin when the baby is still in the cot with the mother or father laying a hand on the baby's head and whispering gently, 'God bless our baby'. It can develop from that to sitting, kneeling or standing beside the one-year-old's bed and saying, for the child to hear, 'Thank you, Father, for taking care of us today. Bless and keep us safe through the night.'

As soon as the child can benefit from a story at bedtime, night prayers can develop to include more of the family: 'Dear God, please bless Martin who came to play today. Please bless too my brothers and sisters, my mummy and daddy, grandma and grandad. Please take care of me while I am asleep. Amen.'

In time other concerns can be included in such prayers. Formal prayers like the 'Our Father' and 'Hail Mary' should not be introduced before the age of six, otherwise these may become nothing more than a chanted rhyme which might stand in the way of the child really learning to pray. All traditional Catholic prayers can and should be taught to the children, but only gradually and as they are old enough to understand the content of the prayer.

While it is nice to get the child to close their eyes and join their hands for prayer, there is no need to insist upon it. It is much better for the whole thing to be as natural and relaxed as possible.

Keep going!

After making a resolute start the most important thing is to keep going! As with so many things where children are concerned, the motto should be 'little and often'. The grace at mealtimes need only be short and to the point and night prayers need not take long, but they must happen every day.

Prayer is rather like a young house plant: if it is not watered regularly it withers and dies, but if it is cared for, it will grow and beautify the house with its flowers. Prayer can only grow in people by regular practice, but the effort is well rewarded. The daily talking with God beautifies a person's character and personality.

Enjoyable

Praying as a family group must never be allowed to become a boring chore. If it begins to fall into a dreary rut, think up ways of enlivening it. Try new approaches: read short passages from the Bible; use a book of prayers; listen to a piece of music; sing a hymn or a folk song. Any method is valid if it helps to improve the quality of your praying. If necessary, as a last resort, stop prayers for a few days or even weeks, then make a fresh start. The only danger with that is the possibility that you will never get back to praying together.

When the children declare, 'I don't want to do it . . . it's boring', that is not the signal for the parents to start insisting, but to ask themselves, 'Are we really getting into a rut? Should we try something new?'

A priest once asked a little boy, 'Do you say your prayers every night, Jimmy?'

'Yes, Father,' Jimmy replied.

'And do you always say them in the morning, too?'

'No, Father, I ain't scared in the daytime!'

Our prayers should spring from our love of God, not from fear. And God, who is always present, hearing and seeing all we do, does not need us to use any special pious words and language when we turn our thoughts to him. All he wants are our hearts and minds raised to him in love.

Earlier generations of Catholics grew up with a different attitude to prayer, repeating faithfully but mechanically the same words every night. This resulted in a rhyming, sing-song manner of saying prayers, rather like magical incantations!

Unfortunately that way of doing things carried with it a kind of superstitious fear. If some of the words were missed out or you forgot to say night prayers, you felt a nagging anxiety something might happen to you!

We have a much more relaxed and healthy understanding nowadays. We know that talking to God – and listening to him – should be a natural part of our daily lives. There is no need for special pious language, dramatic gestures or posture.

Everything can and should be a matter for prayer:

- if the children find a ladybird, they can draw it and praise God for its beauty
- if the boy next door has an accident, we can ask God to make him better
- if an auntie has a new baby we can thank God

and so on.

Posture

The old catechism used to say that praying was 'raising the mind and heart to God'. That is just what it is. You can do that just as well whether you are sitting, standing, walking, lying in bed or kneeling. The advantage of introducing prayer to children while they are holding hands round the table or lying in bed is that they learn, indirectly, that a special posture is not necessary. Hopefully this will mean that the children will grow up to feel that it is quite natural to pray to their heavenly Father on the bus, in the bath, in the classroom or wherever they find themselves with a quiet moment.

Traditional prayers

There is a difference between 'praying' and 'saying prayers'. The first consists of spontaneous little chats with God. In time these might grow to be very simply 'a raising of the heart and mind to God', without using any particular words. The second means using those important set prayers or formulae which have been handed down to us over the centuries.

The Lord's Prayer is, of course, the most important of these because it contains the words of Jesus himself. The 'Hail Mary' must come next because it, too, has its roots in Scripture. These are the most important. The 'I believe', Memorare and others should also be taught to the children, but only when they are ready for them. One of the best ways to do this is to add a part of the Lord's Prayer or 'Hail Mary' to night prayers and gradually introduce the prayer phrase by phrase. To teach the whole prayer right off tends to lead to a parrot-like repetition of words which might not be understood.

The rosary

'And what', the pious old parish priest asked the class of seven-year-olds, 'do you think Mary was doing when the angel Gabriel came to ask her to be the mother of Jesus?' Overawed by the venerable Irish Father the class was silent. 'Do you think she was reading a comic or lying on the floor watching television?' Silence. 'No, she was down on her knees saying her rosary!'

Well, of course, we have had the rosary a long time – but not that long! The idea of a set of prayers recited while thumbing a string of beads is found in several world religions – Buddhism, Hinduism and Islam. The title for the Christian practice is rather lovely. 'Rosary' comes from the Latin word for 'rose garden'.

The early Christian monks developed a form of the rosary but it was not the rosary of Our Lady as we know it today; that seems to have made its first appearance about the time of St Dominic (who died in 1221). It was not, however, officially approved by the Church until 1552 and remained very popular until the early 1960s.

At one time the public recitation of the rosary formed an important part of parish worship but now it has almost completely disappeared in many places. This does not mean that the Church does not want us to use it privately. It would be a great shame if our children grew up ignorant of how to pray the rosary. Most children still receive a set of rosary beads on their first communion day. That presents the ideal opportunity to show them how to use their gift.

If the family is using the whole or part of the rosary at certain times of the year (May, the month dedicated to Mary, and October, the month of the rosary) then the introduction will happen quite naturally when those times come round. Otherwise night prayer would seem the best time to talk about the use of the beads. A little at a time is best. There is no reason why the prayers cannot be divided up so as to make the whole thing more understandable. It is a love of the rosary we are trying to put across, not a regimented mechanical operation involving counting and repetition.

When a parent is saying a decade of the rosary (one is quite enough to begin with) with a child or the family together, each 'Hail Mary' can be split into its two halves, (the second part starts at 'Holy Mary . . .') with each person or group having half to say. Each decade of the three Mysteries (Joyful, Sorrowful or Glorious) covers a little of the story of Christ's redeeming work and the story can be spread between the prayers. One way is to set the scene before beginning the decade ('Mary was quite young when the angel came to ask her to be the mother of Jesus. Plans were being made by her family for her to marry a carpenter called Joseph.'). After the first two 'Hail Mary's the leader tells a little more of the story. This means, in practice, spreading the story over five little 'tellings', so it has to be done sparingly. As time goes by the children will learn what it means to meditate upon the story.

Keep it simple

Some families successfully turn off the TV set at a definite time each evening and kneel down for family prayers. This is very praiseworthy and excellent, but there are not too many who can do this. Some would feel that it is artificial and tends to put the children off – particularly teenagers. We must never forget that it is the *praying* that counts and the *when* and the *where* and the *how* matter much less. Simplicity is important. The best of all prayers are childlike; a 'Father, we love and trust you' spoken from the heart is of more value than hours of complicated prayer.

Finally
Lent is the ideal time to begin praying as a family and a resolute, determined start is called for. Once the first enthusiasm has worn off it is simply necessary to keep at it. That should not mean developing a boring habit. As much as possible, prayer should be enjoyed by the family, and no effort or method should be spared to keep it alive and interesting. The Church's year, with its festivals and seasons, comes to our aid and helps to keep up our interest with its great variety.

Praying faithfully every day is to live by the Christian virtues of faith, hope and charity.

- It is our *love* of God which prompts us to pray, day after day.
- It is our *faith* which assures us that God is there and hears.
- It is our *hope* that our loving Father will respond. (See 1 John 4:16.)

Chapter 4
Easter
The Triumph of Love

Introductory thoughts

If you wake in the middle of the night and look out of the window, it is almost as though the whole world has closed down. It's dark and silent – as silent as the grave. For the sick, nights can be long and very trying, but there is always the hope of the coming of light and the dawning of a new day.

If you take a country walk in mid-winter, the trees seem dead and the countryside is bleak, but there is the hope and happiness of spring to look forward to. When someone we love dies, everything seems to close down – it seems to be night time and winter time all rolled into one. But our Christian faith tells us at such a time that there is life after death; the light and happiness of a future resurrection gives us hope.

- At the dawn of each day light triumphs over darkness.
- Each year spring triumphs over winter.
- In every person's life love can triumph over death.

In the first two, nature takes its course; in the third the co-operation of the human person is required. Love *can* triumph if it springs from a lively faith. And the basis of that faith is Christ's own triumph over suffering and death.

At the time of Jesus and throughout the lives of the apostles, the Roman Empire, which was the political power in their lives, celebrated 'triumphs'. When a general returned to Rome after a great land or sea victory there was a massive triumphal procession through the streets of Rome. The victorious general's chariot was decorated with wreaths of laurel announcing that he was the victor.

The early Christians did not hang up crucifixes in their homes as we do. When they portrayed the cross it was without the naked figure of Christ. It was shown as a triumphant sign with a laurel wreath around it. Christ had died but had risen victorious – Christ, the victor over death.

Our drawing shows the victor's laurels surmounting the cross and round the CHI-RHO sign. That comes from the Greek letters Xp (in English CHR) and is shorthand for Christ. So the picture – from a fourth-century sculpture – says, 'Christ, the victor, has triumphed over the cross'.

Escape stories

A very good preparation for the children's understanding of Holy Week and the 'passover' of Jesus is a good escape story; an escape from imprisonment to freedom. Sometimes newspapers carry such stories, often with accompanying pictures and drawings. A popular Second World War film, *The Great Escape*, tells the story of how determined British soldiers and airmen tunnelled under a wire fence to escape imprisonment. The following story describes an escape to freedom over the Berlin Wall in the 1970s:

> John and Michael were well aware that over seventy people had been killed trying to escape over the Berlin Wall but they were determined to try. With the help of a friend who lived in West Berlin they worked out a plan.

EASTER

First they searched for a tall block of flats on their side of the wall. It had to face a house that was not quite so tall on the west side of the wall. When they had found number five Schmoller Strasse, they needed a fibreglass bow, steel arrows, 100 metres of fishing line and some quarter-inch steel wire.

They hid in the top of the house for fifteen hours until conditions were just right. At 5am a signal flashed by torch from the house on the other side. They opened a window and fired the arrow with the line attached over the house opposite. The arrow sailed over the house to where their friend was waiting. He pulled in the line with the cable attached to it and secured it to the back of his car. Each of the escapers had to wait for the moment when the Communist guards in their observation towers were looking the other way. Then, hitched to a pulley made to run down the wire, Michael, followed by John, sailed over the 'death wall' to the house on the other side, passing over from the closed-in unhappiness of East Berlin to joy and freedom in the West.

It was very like the great escape of the Israelites from the slavery of Egypt. That event has been celebrated by the Jewish people every year since it happened, right up to this day. This escape story could be used in discussion with the family, although basing the discussion on a topical story straight from the newspaper would be better. To help get the idea of 'passover' across to the younger family members it might be useful to make a chart, something like this.

John and Michael feel closed in and unhappy in East Berlin	Escape over the 'death wall'	Freedom and new life in the West
Moses and Israelites very unhappy slaves in Egypt	Escape through the waters of 'Sea of Reeds'	Freedom and new life in Promised Land
Jesus unhappy at our slavery to sin	Escape for us through Jesus' death	Freedom from effects of original sin – new life as children of God

You can well imagine John and Michael's joy and excitement at escaping and how they would celebrate every year the anniversary of their escape, their 'passing over' the 'death wall'. So every year the Jewish people celebrate their 'passing over' all those centuries ago. It is important for an understanding of so much in the Christian way of life (especially baptism and the Mass) to realise that it was on the very festival of the Passover that Jesus went out to his death and passed over to the risen life.

THE THREE SPECIAL DAYS

Every effort should be made by the whole family to attend the liturgy on these special days – the highlight of the Church's year.

HOLY THURSDAY (OR MAUNDY THURSDAY)

As a devout Jew, Jesus celebrated the Jewish festival of Passover. At his last Passover he gave us, for the very first time, the sacrament and sacrifice of the Eucharist. By so doing he placed himself forever at our service.

The liturgy on this evening falls into three dramatic acts:

1. After the Gospel story of Jesus washing the feet of his friends the priest washes the feet of a number of volunteers.
2. We recall that this Eucharist celebrates the very first time Jesus gave himself in this way.
3. The altars are stripped.

If your family cannot attend the evening liturgy, then before the evening meal you could have an extended grace, your own little service. This would, of course, be adapted according to the ages of those present.

After the sign of the cross, Mum or Dad can ask one of the children, 'What is special about today? What happened on the first Maundy Thursday?' Trying to build on the answer, whatever it might be, Mum or Dad continues, 'In the Church this evening three important things happen. Everyone there will remember the first time Jesus gave himself to us in Holy Communion. They will also remember something else that he did. It was to show us that Holy Communion isn't something just for ourselves.

'He got up from the table (*if Mum is speaking then Dad can get up – this is especially easy if the family is eating in the kitchen and can match the words with actions*), filled a bowl with water and put a towel over his arm. Then he went round and washed the feet of his friends – including Judas who was just about to go out and betray him.' (*The parent with bowl and towel may match actions with words and take off socks and briefly wash the family's feet.*)

When the parent has sat down: 'Only after Jesus had shown his love in this way, by serving his friends, did he take the bread, bless it and give it to them.'

The little service can finish with a simple prayer such as:

We thank you, Lord Jesus,
for your example of humble service
and for the gift of yourself in the Eucharist,
the breaking of bread.
May we follow your example of loving service
by helping one another.
May we always be grateful
for all the gifts we receive from you. Amen.

GOOD FRIDAY

For the modern Christian family there is a certain tension between Good Friday as the 'holy day' and as the public holiday. On the only other occasion when a sacred day and a secular holiday come together – Christmas Day – everyone is more or less in step. However, on Good Friday the secular world is coolly indifferent to the sacred meaning of the day. If parents are serious about the Faith then there will be no question about where the emphasis will be. From the very beginning of the day it should be experienced by the family as different and special.

Good Friday breakfast

Lots of families replace their breakfast toast on this day with toasted hot cross buns. As it is a bank holiday, with a little organisation the family can all eat breakfast together. Whoever leads the grace should draw everyone's attention to the hot cross buns with some suitable comment, for example:

> Dear Father,
> even the food we eat today
> reminds us how special and important this day is.
> Your Son's great love and obedience
> took him to death on the cross;
> please deepen our love of you
> and help us to be obedient to your commandments.
> May we always be grateful for the food we eat
> and all the gifts you give us.
> We ask this through Jesus,
> who lives and reigns now and for ever. Amen.

While we recall what happened on the first Good Friday so that we may better appreciate Jesus' great love for us, we must keep in mind that Jesus is with us here and now. His resurrection gave us his continuing presence for ever. So, while we recall the sad events of that day and express sorrow for our sin, we must remember that we have him with us even as we recall those events!

Way of the Cross

Today, in some form or other, the story of Jesus' passion should be followed in a devotional way. It is true that the family will hear the Passion read at the afternoon liturgy, but something additional might be attempted. This could be:

- a service of the Way of the Cross, arranged in the parish church
- a family version of the Way of the Cross (see page 51)
- a public procession of witness
- a simple retelling by parents for their children.

Those who have lived through the cold and gloom of winter really appreciate the beauty of spring. Those who have suffered the loneliness of a wakeful night greet the morning light with relief and joy.

In a similar way only those who have taken Lent seriously and died spiritually with Christ on Good Friday can experience the resurrection joy of Easter.

A public procession of witness

In some places a united procession of witness is organised on Good Friday by the local Churches. It usually involves the carrying of a large wooden cross through the streets in the middle of the day. Sometimes the procession takes the form of a Way of the Cross, with regular stops for a meditation on the Passion, a Scripture reading and a prayer. Not everyone finds it easy to take part but it really is a terrific opportunity for the family to proclaim their Faith. It is a wonderful annual lesson for the children, showing them the need to be courageous in witnessing to their Faith.

Telling the story

It is hard to improve upon an old-fashioned recounting of the Passion in one's own words. As the story is one of supreme love and sacrifice it is very fitting for it to be told in a family group. Mum or Dad knows enough of the story to put it across without having to read it (the Gospel Passion will be read during the afternoon liturgy).

Pictures are a different matter. They are a great help to both the parent in telling the story and the children in listening. One of the best sets of pictures available is those from the film *Jesus of Nazareth*. They can be obtained as slides, but the book of the same name – the text is by William Barclay – has over twenty excellent pictures on the Passion. Remind the children, before showing them the photographs, that these are not real photos of Jesus and his friends but pictures from a film. After the 'telling' – and naturally the inevitable questions – the younger members can be encouraged to draw a picture or use playdough or building bricks to depict a part of the story.

Family fast day

For the adults, Good Friday is a day of fasting and abstinence. But there is no more suitable day in the year for the whole family to do without a little. Before the main meal of the day the grace should reflect this:

> Almighty Father,
> today we are thinking
> about the wonderful love of your Son
> which took him to the cross.
> That love reminds us
> that we often fail in our loving.
> To express our sorrow
> for the hurt we have caused you
> we are trying to do without a little today.
> Please accept the love
> we are trying to express in this way
> and may the money we save
> and give to the needy uplift them a little.
> We thank you for all the good things
> we have received from your hand,
> especially the food we are about to share. Amen.

HOLY SATURDAY

Easter decorations

Children, especially young ones, learn better through what is seen taking place in the home than by words spoken at school, at church or even in the home. So to help the children look forward eagerly to Easter – as indeed they do to Christmas – things need to happen and be seen to happen!

We have no tradition in this country of decorating our homes for Easter but there is no reason why we cannot start our own family tradition. Children are never going to discover the importance of Easter as the pinnacle of the

Church's year if it remains uncelebrated in the home. With the season of spring reflecting the theme of new life, the ideal preparation is to take a walk in the countryside or perhaps a park. Primary school children will almost certainly have been talking about spring and new life at school. But pre-school children too will take delight in being shown the daffodils in flower and the new fresh green buds appearing on the trees and bushes.

A few bunches of daffodils arranged with a selection of twigs in bud collected on your county walk (not from the park, of course!) make a simple and effective arrangement. The children are usually on school holidays for a few days before the festival and can be organised to decorate the house in fitting fashion. Most young children like to have the opportunity to show off their drawing and painting skills. Scenes from nature, showing new life appearing, pictures of Easter eggs, pictures of the open tomb, of Jesus appearing to his friends – there are plenty of subjects. But definitely no Easter bunnies! They have absolutely no relevance to or connection with Easter.

The emphasis of the pictures should be joyful and positive, but if a child insists on drawing a crucifixion scene, use it as an opportunity to talk about the death of Jesus. Take care to emphasise that the sad part, when Jesus seemed to be beaten by death, was followed by the most important part of all – his coming alive in a new and special way. That new way of living makes it possible for him to be with us now and for ever as our friend. Then encourage the young artist to show the victory of Christ by adding yellow and orange rays shining out from the cross to all parts of the world.

Easter candles

In some primary schools children learn how to make Easter candles from paper. These are extremely simple and most appealing. Any home could make a number to stand among the flowers on the mantelpiece, or the window sill. They can be as large or small as the paper supply allows.

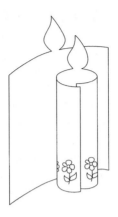

While the smaller candles appeal especially to the five- to eight-year-olds, the older children might like to co-operate on a larger project – a huge family Easter candle. Most households have a half-used roll of wallpaper in the attic, garage or understairs cupboard (if not, a neighbour will surely help). The idea is identical to the above, except this one is to be 4 or 5 feet tall and made to stand on its own in a dignified corner of the living room, lounge or hallway. It might be best placed in a decorated tub or box. If older children are involved the candle should bear a closer resemblance to the Easter candle in the parish church, by adding a decorated A and Ω (Alpha and Omega) and the year's date.

Easter cards

If we are serious about the importance of Easter and what it means, we should make an effort to send cards. There is never a very good selection in the shops for the obvious reason that there is little demand! The children could use their leisure time and talent throughout Holy Week to produce homemade ones.

Easter eggs

If it were not for Easter eggs, most children would not realise that there was anything special about the Easter bank holiday weekend. At first glance eggs seem to have no link with Our

Lord's death and resurrection but in fact they can be a most useful teaching aid. The first and most important rule about Easter eggs and their symbolism is that within the family no Easter eggs are to be given or eaten before Easter Day. (The 'Day' – 'this is the day the Lord has made' – begins with the end of the Easter vigil.) Families with young children tend to produce the eggs *after* breakfast (for obvious reasons!) on Easter morning. After breakfast, which should ideally be of boiled eggs, Mum and Dad can make something of the occasion by presenting the eggs with an accompanying explanation of their symbolism.

The adult needs only an ordinary hen's egg (hard boiled) to illustrate the explanation, and can follow the general outline of the following:

'Why do we have chocolate eggs as a present today?' (Even if an older child remembers a previous year's explanation and gives a correct answer, still proceed with the following for the sake of any younger child.)

'Can you imagine for a moment a space ship landing from outer space? The landing site it chooses is a wide, pebbly beach. After a few minutes a hatch opens and out steps a strange-looking little space traveller. He looks around at the scenery. There's no one in sight. Bending down, he picks up one of the round/oval stones. He weighs it in his hands, then tests it with a little calculator-like box in his left hand. It's smooth, cold and lifeless. He looks around at a beach full of lifeless stones. Our space traveller walks up the beach to a bank of grass. After inspecting that, he sees in the distance a farmhouse and its barns and outhouses. He walks cautiously towards the buildings. Halfway there he almost steps on a cluster of brown, oval, stone-like objects. "More stones," he thinks, but when he picks one up it's warm. He runs his little machine over it and finds, to his surprise, that there is life inside what looks and feels like a stone.' (The storyteller now shows the egg in their hand and says, 'Eggs really do look and feel like stones.')

'As the space traveller holds the egg in his hand it cracks, once, twice, three times, and as he watches, a little chick pushes its head out into the world. You can imagine the surprise of the space traveller; new life from what looked like a stone. It is a perfect example of what happened on the first Easter morning. The stone, behind which Jesus had been buried, looked cold and dead, but suddenly new life burst out of it – Jesus was alive. The risen Jesus came out of what seemed a cold, dead stone to new life.'

Such a story can bring out the symbolism and relevance of the chocolate Easter egg.

EASTER DAY

'This is the day,' we sing on Easter Sunday. The day of love's triumph over sin and death. Everything about Easter Sunday speaks of triumph. Eastern Christians call it that 'unique and holy day, king and lord of days, feast of feasts, solemnity of solemnities'. It is so important a day for Christians that, having prepared for it for forty days, the next forty days are spent celebrating it! From Easter Sunday until Ascension Day, 'Alleliua' is our song as 'the day' is continually celebrated. When those forty days are up, the celebration of Our Lord's resurrection continues – every Sunday: the first day of the week is our weekly remembrance of the day he rose.

There is a neat catch question to ask children if you discover that they are learning about the Ten Commandments. You can ask, 'Which of the Ten Commandments do Christians break?' The answer is the fourth commandment, 'Remember to keep holy the Sabbath day'. Those commandments were drawn up for the Jewish people and the fourth one refers to their holy day, which, of course, is Saturday. Jesus said that he had not come to sweep away the Jewish laws, but to fulfil them. This is one example where God still wants us to retain the idea behind the law, but on a different day. Christians, of course, keep Sunday holy, the first day of the week and the day Jesus rose from the dead.

Sundays

With so many jobs to do around the house, outside or on the car, it is difficult for adults to think of Sunday as a 'holy' day. But that is what it is, if being a Christian means anything to us. It is also a family day when families have the opportunity, since they are free from work, to be together and do things together.

There should be two highlights to the day, both to do with 'family'. As members of God's family we meet together with other family members to share a meal, offer a sacrifice and celebrate Jesus' continuing presence with us. Sunday Mass is just that. There are too many of us to get *round* the altar table literally, but that is what we would do if it were possible. We listen to God's word and share from the table of the Lord.

The Passover meal is the centre of the Jewish year – the Last Supper meal of Jesus has become the centre of the week for Christians: 'The Eucharist is a family meeting, a meeting of the large family of Christians. Every altar will always be a table round which gathers a family of brothers and sisters', in the words of Pope John Paul II.

The second highlight of Sunday is our own private family meal together – Sunday dinner. There can be no more important regular family event each week than this. It is so vital to the happy, balanced life of the family that parents should gently but firmly insist that the whole family will always be together for Sunday dinner.

All through human history sharing a meal has always been seen as a very significant event. 'Going out for a meal' is still one of the most accepted ways to celebrate an anniversary or birthday. Think too of wedding receptions, birthday parties, and so on; they all involve a meal and togetherness. In most societies around the globe sharing a meal together denotes special bonds of friendship.

If you want to strengthen your family life then eat together as often as you can – daily if possible. The family table is the place for sharing and serving one another. Talking, sharing ideas, asking advice, passing on news, all take place round the table. It is difficult to think of every Sunday dinner as a celebration but good habits can be formed to make it clearly special and different. If a tablecloth is not used during the week then using one on Sunday will add to the sense of occasion. Laying the place settings with care, arranging a simple flower display or a decorative centrepiece: these simple little things can mark the meal as different.

The resurrection symbols

Here are a few symbols of the resurrection that the children might like to draw, and which give you further opportunity to explain what we are celebrating.

The Butterfly. It is not only children who find it fascinating how the caterpillar goes into a cocoon (a type of tomb) where it seems to die, then emerges to a new life as a beautiful butterfly. It is a terrific symbol of Christ's death and resurrection. Rather than skip over this symbol quickly, it might be an idea to have a more detailed home project based on different butterflies and their life cycles. Don't forget to point out the symbolism; it is a most valuable way of tying in God's creation with his work of re-creation.

The Phoenix. This was a very popular symbol of the resurrection with the early Christians. They used it on burial stones and in their writings. The first Christian writer we know of who used the ancient legend about a mythical bird was Clement of Rome. Around AD 98 he records the legend in his letter to the Corinthian Christians and applies it to the resurrection of all Christ's faithful followers. Later it was applied to Christ's own resurrection.

According to legend, the phoenix was a bird that lived for 500 years, then built itself a funeral pyre for a nest and burnt itself to death. When the ashes cooled, the bird rose again from the ashes to start a new life.

Lamb and Flag. At the time of Jesus lambs were sacrificed in the Jerusalem temple as part of an act of worship. Jesus was described by John the Baptist as 'the Lamb of God': the lamb that would be sacrificed to take away the sins of the world. Only this lamb was victorious, rising to a new life. The standing lamb therefore represents Jesus and the flag is the sign of his triumph.

Easter and 'the teens'

That agonising period of development which we call, in modern jargon, 'the teens', is a time of discovery, and not only for the young person! This time of self-discovery includes searching for what is real and what is true: 'They look for independence and are reluctant to conform. Sometimes they wish to reject past traditions and even reject their faith.' That was Pope John Paul II, speaking at York, on his first visit to Britain. He showed that he knew and appreciated this period of questioning that adolescents have to go through on their way to adulthood.

Parents often feel that they have personally failed if a son or daughter, nurtured in the Faith, suddenly and sullenly refuses to go to Mass. Parents have to be fair to themselves and realise that this rebellion is natural and even quite healthy. Young people need time and support as they sort out priorities in their minds, and find their way to a more mature faith and commitment.

ASCENSION DAY

Although Ascension Day always falls on a Thursday, because it is exactly forty days from Easter Sunday (see Acts 1:3), it is an important, if generally unnoticed, festival. Ascension Day is one of the earliest of the Christian holy days to be celebrated, dating from the late fourth century, well before Christmas Day!

While theologians may debate what actually happened at the Ascension, the meaning is clear; it marks the final appearance of the risen Jesus to his friends, and his return to his Father. That is what we celebrate. For centuries – up until 1970 – this was symbolised by the public extinguishing and removal of the Easter (Paschal) candle from the church (see page 73). While this is no longer done in church, it does suggest an idea for the home. If the Easter candle suggestion (see page 74) was followed, then the candles can be moved onto or near the table for the evening meal. After a suitable grace and a word of explanation, the candle(s) are extinguished – by cutting the flame off with scissors if they are made of paper or card, or blowing out a candle lit especially for the occasion.

Chapter 5
PENTECOST
The Giving of Love

Introductory thoughts

Many families now have home computers. If you want to get the most out of such an electronic device you have to learn basic computer language. You need to understand the symbols and icons used, how to give instructions to the computer and understand what it says.

The same thing goes for learning to drive. If you want to be a competent driver and pass your driving test you must know and understand the road signs. The 'language' of the road consists not just in road signs shown in the Highway Code but also in the experience of how other people drive.

So many 'languages' exist in addition to the obvious spoken word. Another example, from day-to-day relationships between people, is what we call 'body language' – the messages people convey to one another by the way they stand, sit and walk, or what they do. This is particularly true in the family:

> 'Don't you look at me like that!' the parent says to the sullen child.

> 'Stop lounging around and get your bedroom tidied up,' says an exasperated mother to her teenage daughter.

> 'This is for you,' the young child says, handing her mother a dandelion.

In the words of the catchphrase, 'It's not what you do, it's the way that you do it'.

Pride brings disunity
There's a rather neglected little story in the first book of the Bible – Genesis 11:1-9. It goes like this:

> At that time, some while after Noah's rescue through the ark, there was only one language spoken by all the people on earth. Then they had a very proud idea: 'Let's make a name for ourselves by building a town and a tower reaching right up into the heavens.' God, however, was not pleased with their idea and while they were busy building, he confused everything and everyone by giving them many different languages. They stopped building because they could no longer communicate with one another.

From that moment on, the Bible tells us, every tribe and people had their own language. As there was now no single language, God himself used signs and symbols to communicate with the human race. And throughout history that is how God has made himself known – except to a few very special people.

God 'speaks' through signs
Of the signs God has used, fire immediately springs to mind (see page 83) but also the wind. There's the beautiful story of Elijah in 1 Kings 19:9-14. The prophet experiences the presence of God not in a strong wind, nor in the earthquake, nor in lightning but in a gentle breeze!

In our lives today God makes his loving presence and his actions known through the words of Scripture and the sign-language of the sacraments (see page 91). If we want to understand what God is saying to us we must learn what the 'language' means and how to use it.

Each feast has its symbols
Each of the Church's feasts has its symbols and signs. Christmas has the baby, the supreme sign of God's love. Epiphany has the Magi with their gifts, showing that God's love is not just for one group of people but for everyone. Easter has the special candle and the waters of baptism.

Pentecost, described in Acts 2:1-4, is especially rich in God's sign language:

> When Pentecost day came round, they had all met in one room, when suddenly they heard what sounded like a powerful wind from heaven, the noise of which filled the entire house in which they were sitting; and something appeared to them that seemed like tongues of fire; these separated and came to rest on the head of each of them. They were all filled with the Holy Spirit, and began to speak foreign languages as the Spirit gave them the gift of speech.

And, full of energy and courage, the apostles rushed out into the crowded streets to speak about Jesus as Lord and Saviour. All the foreigners from every corner of the Roman Empire, gathered in Jerusalem for the feast of Pentecost, were amazed to find that they could understand what was said. It was the tower of Babel story in reverse! (See page 82.) The Spirit brought unity as the Church began to be built.

The special message of Pentecost
The signs of Pentecost are wind and fire:

> *Wind:* Now that we have the everyday use of electricity, we forget how the wind was once used as a source of energy. Ships were propelled by wind and windmills ground grain and drew up water; so the blowing of the wind was a sign of the arrival of energy and power.

> *Fire:* In our more luxurious lives we fail to realise how important fire was in simpler, more rudimentary times. It was essential for heating, cooking and lighting in the home. It was a symbol of warmth, purification and illumination. Fire also arouses widely different emotions – a cosy glow when seated round an open fire in the winter and terrifying fear when a building catches fire.

At Pentecost the Holy Spirit came as a source of great energy and power and in that power the apostles immediately went out to proclaim Christ. Pentecost, then, is the birthday of the Church and the time when we are all reminded of our Christian call to be missionaries. The apostles were transformed by the coming of the Spirit. The fire symbolised how the Spirit warmed their hearts and cleansed their minds. Suddenly they understood who their friend Jesus really was and what they must do – and out they went to do it.

The Jewish festival of Pentecost

Long before the time of Jesus, the Jewish people had celebrated the feast of Pentecost, as they still do today. It is a celebration of the first picking from the harvest fields – rather like the harvest festival we have later in the year. It is also closely linked to the Passover. After Passover they counted fifty days and on the fiftieth celebrated Pentecost (the word means 'fiftieth' in Greek). It was on that day that the Jewish people celebrated the Covenant (or agreement) that God had made with Moses, their leader. It was the spirit of the Covenant, their loyalty to God, that united them.

The Christian Church actually begins with the 'passover' of Christ at Easter. But only with the coming of the Holy Spirit (while the apostles, as good Jews, were celebrating the Jewish feast) does it really come alive. Pentecost is the completion or fulfilment of Easter. It is always thought of as the birthday of the Church.

'Giving of Love'

Our first chapter, 'The Coming of Love', spoke of the great revelation, through Jesus, that God *is* love. At Christmas we celebrate that wonderful event when God came into our world as one of us. Our second chapter was about the Epiphany and was entitled 'The Showing of Love' because the word Epiphany means 'showing'. The chapter covering Lent and Holy Week was called 'The Offering of Love' because Jesus' love for us prompted him to make the offering of himself on our behalf to the Father. Because the Father accepted his offering, Easter is a time of great triumph. So that chapter was called 'The Triumph of Love'.

This present chapter is entitled 'The Giving of Love' because true love shows itself in its impulse to give, and perfect love gives perfectly and completely.

The Holy Spirit is understood to be the spirit of love between the Father and the Son in the intimate love of the mysterious Holy Trinity. It was the giving of that same spirit of love that instantly transformed fearful men into energetic preachers and missionaries. It was the fire of love given to their hearts that warmed them and burned out of their minds their misunderstandings about Jesus and his message.

The neglected festival

As the fulfilment of Easter and the birthday of the Church, this day is one of the most important in the year. It is certainly more important than Christmas, yet it is rather neglected. This might be because of the time of the year – warmer weather and holidays in the air; it might be because the symbols of the feast are not so easy to understand; it could be because the secular bank holiday weekend of Whitsun gets confused with the Christian Whit Sunday, or it may be because its importance has never properly been understood and no tradition has been built up. For whatever reason, Pentecost tends to get overlooked. Our parish churches could do more to mark the Church's birthday and to encourage the celebration of the occasion in the home.

Practical suggestions

Which name, Whitsun or Pentecost?

A worthwhile little project to set the children as part of their preparation for Pentecost is to ask them to find out – from school or their local priest, from the library or books around the home – what is the meaning of the two names given to this time in the Church's year. It is amazing how few

Catholics know what either word means or how to use it.

First, it has to be said that both titles do apply to the self-same day. As we said above, the name 'Pentecost' comes from the Jewish tradition and means 'fiftieth day' since the Passover. The word 'Whitsun' is a shortening of 'Whitsunday' and is totally of Christian origin. In the early Church the period from Easter to Pentecost, during which Easter continued to be celebrated, was the time when people who had prepared throughout Lent to be received into the Christian community were baptised.

In our part of the world, Northern Europe, it became more common and popular to have the baptisms at or near Pentecost day. (This may have been because of the climate – the candidates for baptism had to strip off! see page 90.) In England the feast became known as 'White Sunday'. This was because of the white clothes worn after their baptising by the newly received converts. Naturally in time this was broken down to 'Whit Sunday' and 'Whitsun'.

Children and symbols

Pentecost is a perfect time to introduce or reintroduce the children to signs and symbols. Here are some symbols that are associated with the festival. Get the children to draw and colour them.

The Descending Dove. This symbol is associated with the times the Holy Spirit appeared during our Lord's life, for example at his baptism (Matthew 3:16).

Tongues of Fire. Seven are drawn to symbolise the seven gifts of the Holy Spirit that are a result of his coming (Acts 2:1-4).

 *Windmill.* The wind is not easy to illustrate but the children might like to draw a windmill, or instead make this paper windmill. It could be decorated with the two symbols from above.

Love is

As Pentecost is the time when we recall the giving of the Spirit of Love to the Church, the table prayer for the principal meal can be based on the theme of love in the family. You have probably seen cartoon pictures and cards captioned, 'Love is . . .' Examples are:

> 'Love is sharing problems with each other,'
> with a picture of Daddy and Mummy sitting talking.

> 'Love is giving the children swimming lessons,'
> with a drawing of Daddy holding a child up in the water at the local pool, while another child sits on the edge.

It might be possible to acquire two or three suitable samples. Show them to the family in the week before Whitsun and suggest that they draw a picture for each member of the family on this theme of love. For example, one of the children might draw Mum cuddling a child with the caption, 'Love is giving us a cuddle when we don't feel very well.' Or for Dad there might be a picture of a car with two feet sticking out from underneath, with the words, 'Love is making the car safe for us all'. Mum and Dad could enter into the fun and draw a suitable picture (matchstick people are good enough!) for each of the family. The cartoons are hidden until the morning of Pentecost day, and then placed, folded, at each person's place for breakfast. The grace might be something like:

> Today we recall that wonderful moment
> when the Holy Spirit, the Spirit of Love,
> came upon the apostles.
> They were filled with energy and fired by love.

May that same Spirit fill us with energy
in God's service and love for one another.

Then everyone opens up their pictures and enjoys a laugh when the secrets are revealed! The cartoons might be used to decorate the kitchen for the following week and be a talking point for neighbours and friends who call.

Children love candles and especially blowing them out. Later in the day at the principal meal – if candles are available – everyone can have one by their place at table. At grace time Mum or Dad says something along these lines:

> At birthday parties there's usually a birthday cake with candles. Today is the birthday of the Church. When we were baptised we became God's people, members of his Church. We are the Church and the candles in front of us are like the ones we were each given when we were baptised. Today it is a birthday candle. (*The candles can now be lit.*) Your candle flames are like the tongues of fire which were seen over the heads of the apostles on the first Pentecost day. Let us be quiet, just for a moment, and ask the Holy Spirit to come and fill our hearts with the fire of his love. (*Short pause.*) Now let's blow out our candles.
>
> When the apostles had received the Holy Spirit they rushed out to tell everyone about Jesus. We are missionaries, too, and in our own little way we must try and make God's love known. So now we say, 'Thank you, God, for the love we share in this home and family. Thank you, too, for the food which comes from your loving hand.' Amen.

If Mum has led the above, Dad might like to finish off with a reading of the following passage. If Dad led the table prayer, perhaps the eldest child could read it. (It's not appropriate for Mum to read it out!) It needs to be introduced with a remark like, 'A 14-year-old girl was asked at school to write about a missionary she knew, and this is what she wrote':

A missionary I know

When I was asked to write about a missionary I knew, a few people crossed my mind, such as Mother Teresa. Then I stopped and thought, 'I can't write about one of these great people because I don't really know them. It's true I've heard their names and read and been told about them, but I don't know what they're like.'

The person I think is a missionary, and a good one, is my mother. This may sound peculiar but surely you don't have to be ordained to be a missionary. My mum's mission is to be a housewife and a mother to me and my family. My mum has never been selfish and put herself first before her family. I have never been starved or been without her endless love. Just like the famous missionaries, my mother has needed a lot of courage. She could easily have gone off shopping or to a party with friends and left me, but she didn't. She made the supreme sacrifice of thinking about me before herself. I am very lucky to have a missionary mother.

If there are teenage children in the family an interesting exchange of ideas might develop over the meal after that school essay!

EASTER SACRAMENTS

The special fifty days from Easter to Pentecost is the period when, in the early centuries of the Christian Church, the three sacraments of baptism, confirmation and holy communion were received by the new converts. Nowadays those who have completed the Rite of Christian Initiation of Adults (RCIA) course in the parish are received into the community at the Easter Vigil. Baptism we have spoken repeatedly about, because it is so important.

Confirmation

'They can't leave anything alone, can they! I don't know what they're doing to confirmation but when I was a youngster the bishop came round every three years and we were confirmed when we were 8 or 9.'

There has definitely been a re-evaluation in the Church about confirmation, and in fact the evaluating goes on! The sacrament is now delayed till an age when young people can understand more fully what it is all about and decide for themselves whether they want to be adult members of the Church. Confirmation, as we shall see, completes baptism. Though the baby could not make a personal commitment, the young person can.

Confirmation in the Early Church

The changes we have seen in recent years arise from a better understanding of how the sacrament fitted into the order of things in the Early Church. Quite simply, Lent was used as the time for preparing the new converts to the Church. When they had been instructed and prepared, they were received into the community. This would have been on Easter Night or during the fifty days that followed. But they were not just baptised, they were also confirmed and made their first holy communion, all at the same special occasion. That seems rather odd to us because we have been brought up with the practice that evolved much later, in the Middle Ages. In the first three to four hundred years of the Church's life the order of events went something like this: The baptism was conducted privately, apart from where the congregation were gathered, because the person entered the water naked. The new convert was then anointed with oil and given special new white clothes on leaving the water. New Christians were then taken to the assembled congregation and presented to the community as its new members, to be given a rousing welcome. The bishop, who would have been presiding, formally received the new members by laying his hands on their heads. While doing this he prayed that they would receive an outpouring of the Holy Spirit. This was followed by an anointing of their heads to show that they now belonged to Christ (the word 'Christ' means 'the anointed one') and were 'Christians'. Then everyone present would celebrate the eucharist and the new Christians received holy communion for the first time.

In time this 'confirming' ceremony became the separate sacrament of confirmation. The two sacraments became separated in time when the practice of baptising babies developed.

Notice the sign-language of confirmation – the laying on of hands by the bishop and the sign of the cross with the holy oil. The first was used by the great figures of Old Testament times, such as Abraham and Isaac, who used to pass on a blessing to their sons with laying-on of hands. At the time of Jesus, a religious teacher would lay his hands on the heads of those he was about to send out to teach.

The sign language of the sacraments

As the risen Jesus, alive and with us, is not visible, we need clear signs to show when he is touching our lives in a special way. For example, the way Christ can act as our daily strength comes across clearly in our receiving the bread (and when possible the wine) of holy communion. That is a sign that actually contains what it is signifying.

The waters of baptism convey the idea of washing clean, but also of the giving of new life. The anointing with oil in baptism, confirmation, holy orders and in the sacrament for the sick is a sign of being made 'special' or set apart. In Old Testament times only priests and kings were anointed in such a way. And, of course, Jesus received the title of 'the Christ', which means 'the anointed one'. Being a 'Christ-ian' sets us apart in the world, with a special task to witness to Christ (hence the importance of things like the procession of witness on Good Friday (see page 71).

Sacraments in the family

None of the sacraments is a purely private meeting with Christ. They involve us all as members of God's family. That is why, when a child receives the sacrament of penance for the first time, or holy communion or confirmation, the preparation and the celebration must be, as much as possible, a family event.

When a child is to be brought for baptism, the parents need to think about the meaning of the sign language of that sacrament, and be clear about the responsibilities they are taking on. Later, when the same child is receiving the sacraments of holy communion and confirmation that fulfil baptism, the family again needs to be fully involved. They will be complementing what the school and the parish are doing to explain the meaning of the 'language' to the child. Most parishes now have schemes which set out to involve the parents and help the child continue to develop and grow in Christian knowledge after the sacraments have been received.

MARY, THE MOTHER OF THE CHURCH

Luke, who wrote the Acts of the Apostles, tells us that Mary, the mother of Jesus, was present in the upper room when the Holy Spirit came. It was very fitting that she, who had given birth to the Saviour, should be present at the birth of the Church, through which we would meet the Saviour. This is probably why Mary was declared, at the time of the Second Vatican Council, the Mother of the Church.

Much of the fifty-day period following Easter falls in May, which has been regarded for centuries as Mary's month. Many grandparents will remember the May processions that were held in most parishes up until the early 1960s. The processions were held outdoors, often through the streets of the parish, carrying a large statue of Mary, with the public recitation of the rosary and Marian hymns. At that time it was common for children to have their own little May altars in the home. There would be a statue of Our Lady in front of which was arranged a simple bouquet of flowers.

Whatever the value of the outdoor processions, there is no doubt that the children's devotion and love and respect for Mary during May was valuable and to be encouraged. This is something we would do well to continue and can be so easily arranged. The children will love finding and arranging flowers for their 'altar'. It is another 'occasion' and opportunity for prayer together. A decade of the rosary, in the simple way already explained (see page 62), would flow naturally and valuably.

TRINITY SUNDAY

The first Sunday after Pentecost is called Trinity Sunday. The feast dates from the Middle Ages and has been particularly popular in England since the time of St Thomas à Becket.

Remembering that we were each baptised 'in the name of the Father and of the Son and of the Holy Spirit', and that we usually commence our prayer with the sign of the cross and those words, in the family we might like to try the following to mark the day. At Sunday dinner, or the meal when the family are together, place a suitable small bowl full of water in the centre of the table. The parent who is going to lead the grace before the meal draws the bowl to the attention of everyone and in a few simple words reminds the family of the Christian significance of water as the sign of new life. A blessing can be asked on the water. These words might be appropriate:

> Almighty God,
> we recall today that you have revealed yourself
> to us as a trinity of persons – Father, Son and Holy Spirit.
> We ask your blessing on this water;
> may it remind us of our baptism
> and the promises made at that time
> to reject evil and to love and dedicate ourselves
> to the good. Amen.

The parent then asks each member of the family to make a sign of the Trinity with the thumb and first two fingers of the right hand. Each of those round the table can then form a 'clover' figure of three, and dip the three fingers into the water and make the sign of the cross, with the usual accompanying words.

Chapter 6
TIME AFTER PENTECOST
The Living of Love

'If you do that once more I'll . . .'
'How many times must I tell you . . .'

Living out love in the family is a constant uphill struggle! Clearing up after the children, keeping after them to get ready, get washed and get a move on, sorting out their squabbles, tolerating their noise and so on and so on! No other way of life offers so much aggravation and temptation nor, on the other hand, such an opportunity to grow in patience and maturity. It is a giving of oneself, and giving and more giving. Looked at positively, it is an opportunity for a steady growth in unselfish love. The words of an old song come to mind:

'Love is something if you give it away,
give it away, give it away.
Love is something if you give it away,
you end up having more.'

Marriage and family life offer just as many opportunities for holiness as any other way of life – some would say many more! As Pope John Paul II has said, 'Christian marriage is the pathway to holiness for all members of a family'.

Night feeds, getting in and out of bed countless times and stumbling around in semi-darkness to attend a sick or restless child, can be a crucifying experience, especially if it goes on night after night for months on end. But it is an experience that is at the very heart of Christianity. It is a living out of the Easter theme of dying to oneself in the service of others.

To give time to another person is to give something of oneself because we have nothing more precious to give. 'Whatever you do for the least person you do for me,' Jesus said. Therefore to help and serve one another in the family is to do things for Christ himself. When things are going badly it helps to take a short moment of quiet to recall that every effort in love for the family is an effort and a mark of love for Christ.

When Pope John Paul II said, 'We are the Easter people,' he was saying that our faith is built on the resurrection of Jesus, but more than this, he was saying that it is the Easter event that makes sense of life; what is important is not just what we believe but how we live each day. All day long families have difficulties and problems and come through them: 'I can't find my school tie'; 'I've backed the car into the garage wall!' 'I think I've got the flu.' We squabble and fall into sin, and then we are reconciled with God and one another. If we have the eyes of faith to see it, life is filled with the continual cycle of 'death and resurrection' and the sustaining love of the risen Jesus.

Re-creation and love

Time is God's precious gift to us. It is vital for the growth of family togetherness that as much time as possible be spent together. Naturally this means making the most of weekends and especially holidays. Everyone needs some kind of break from daily routine for a rest and a change. Only by breaking the familiar pattern of daily life can we get a sense of re-creation, of an opportunity for the family to be united in common interests and have fun together.

Only by being in one another's company continuously for a week or two can there be sufficient opportunity for the growth in love that comes from sharing. Not only is it important for each member of the family to give and share love but equally it is important for each member to feel that they are loved – to discover that they are lovable. No one is able to discover this all by themselves. While this holds true for everyone, it is particularly important for the teenager.

Within the family no masks need to be worn, no dramatic act is required, no pretence is expected. Everyone can be themselves, always welcomed and loved. This is one of the gifts of the Holy Spirit to the family, the ability to make each other feel special in spite of any recurring bad behaviour or weakness. To 're-create' together is to help the 'specialness' grow. The summer holidays provide a wonderful opportunity for this, when everyone has more leisure and time for one another.

Saints' time

Through the summer months, in the Church's liturgy we are continually looking back through Pentecost to Easter. This is the time of the year when we remember the saints, those members of the family of God who lived heroic lives of love and are now with God. We are still struggling to live a life of love but saints are people who have struggled and with God's grace succeeded. Moreover, they are now in a position to help us live the same life.

Young people need mature, unselfish adults to look up to and admire, and this is always a challenge to parents. But they also need heroes from outside their family. The summer holidays provide an opportunity to introduce the family to the Christian heroes of the past. One way is to encourage summer holiday reading based on the lives of the saints – the more exciting ones, of course!

> The story goes that a little girl was with her family in a group being shown around one of our great cathedrals. As the guide was explaining a historic tomb nearby, the girl was staring at a great stained-glass window, through which the summer sun was streaming, bathing the cathedral floor in colour. As the group was about to move on she asked the guide in a shrill clear voice, 'Who are those people in the pretty window?'
>
> 'Those are the saints,' the man replied.
>
> That night, as she was undressing for bed, she told her mother, 'I know who the saints are.'
>
> 'Do you, dear?' replied her mother. 'Who are they?'
>
> 'They're the people who let the light shine through.'

What a perfect way of describing the saints. They are the people through whom the light of God's immense love shines out on others.

In the local church

It is easy to attend the same church week after week and take for granted what is in it, accepting it as part of the décor. Sometimes there are statues of saints which are never explained to children, most likely because the adults don't know much about them either! Nowadays there are fewer statues in our churches but, where they exist, the children of the parish should grow up knowing about them. This is particularly true of the parish's patron saint. The children should be encouraged to ask questions. Why, for example, do we consider St Thérèse of Lisieux a saint? What did St John Fisher or St Thomas More do to merit sainthood? What can we learn about living the life of love from their lives? These are questions that the parish clergy and teachers can help parents with, and ideal material for a home-based project.

Holiday expeditions

Our great cathedrals are obvious places for a family visit, but old parish churches (the principal Anglican church in each town or village) are also worth considering. If the weather is bad while on holiday, why not seize the opportunity to explore the neighbourhood and look out for one of the old pre-Reformation parish churches? Every village and town has its Anglican parish church, most of which were originally built as Catholic churches and used for centuries by Catholics.

While the children might find the idea of visiting old churches a bit 'boring', it can be made interesting. Encourage them to imagine the travelling craftsmen, called journeymen, who with great skill carved the wood and worked the stone for the churches. Describe to them the streams of people, in the various period costumes, coming and going for weddings, baptisms and funerals. Suggest they explore the church (in a dignified way) and find which parts are the really old bits (many churches were extended or partially rebuilt over the centuries). They can look for the clues which tell you that in this particular church Mass used to be said. One of the sure signs is the existence of a piscina on the right-hand side of the altar (as you face it from the body of the church). This was a little saucer-like basin with a drain-hole. Water used at Mass was poured away down this drain.

Our Catholic Christian heritage
Children and young people need to realise that being a Catholic Christian is not just a here-and-now experience. The Catholic community has roots that go way back to the conversion of England, long before AD 1066. We are members of a great spiritual family that includes hundreds of inspiring English saints. There are the ordinary people too, who once used these old churches, and who had their struggles to live a life of love and are now 'saints' with God. They are happy to pray for us who are still struggling. So while we admire the craftsmanship of those long-dead Christians, we should remind the children that the stained-glass windows that they see, the stonework, wall paintings and other beautiful objects were all made with loving care by people who shared the same Faith.

Wall paintings
Children might find it particularly interesting to paint or draw the wall paintings in the old parish churches. The interior of all medieval churches was more or less completely painted. Sadly, so many of these pictures have disappeared, either because they were deliberately destroyed at the Reformation or because they had to come down when the church was altered or enlarged. A number of pictures have survived because they were covered with lime-wash rather than destroyed during the Reformation. More were lost in the time of Queen Victoria because at that time there was a great craze for stripping the plaster walls to show off the original stonework. This was a great mistake because not only were hundreds of wall pictures hidden under lime-wash lost, but

the original stonework was nothing special to look at. The original builders had never intended it to be seen!

The travelling painter of the Middle Ages was commissioned to paint on the walls of the parish church for two reasons, devotional and educational. There were no printed books; the very few that did exist had been copied by hand by the monks. Because of this only about 10 per cent of the population could read. But everyone could understand pictures and the wall pictures were aids in the education of the people. The priest, in his sermon, could point at a picture and speak of the Bible character shown or the saint portrayed. The pictures had to be self-explanatory and were painted with a direct simplicity. The standard of the artist's work was not very high (the better-skilled journeymen were fully employed at the cathedrals) but that didn't matter to the parishioners. The pictures were not intended to last anyway, they could easily be replaced the next time the journeyman came that way again.

There are five basic subjects covered by the pictures:

1. Bible stories
2. Single figures of saints
3. Lives of the saints
4. Moral illustrations
5. Decorative schemes

It has often been said that the people of those early English churches did not know their Bible (relative to the fact there were no printed books and hardly anyone could read) but the surviving wall paintings tell a different story. Scenes from the Bible abound, but they seem to have preferred New Testament stories (rather like modern Catholics!).

The single saints portrayed were, of course, those popular at the time. These were, for example, St Christopher, St Catherine, St Nicholas and St Margaret. The lives of the saints were often portrayed in a series of pictures not unlike our modern strip cartoon. Not surprisingly one of the most popular subjects for these series was Our Lady, to whom devotion was very strong in the Middle Ages.

The wall paintings were also used to warn congregations about the last judgement and the final coming of Christ. The struggle between good and evil, the promise of heaven and the doom awaiting those who die in sin are all clearly spelt out.

Where some of these wall paintings can be seen
If you are on holiday at one of the following seaside resorts you might visit the old parish churches in the nearby village or town.

Hastings: Battle
Brighton: Patcham

There is a Sussex group of churches at Clayton, Plumpton, Hardham and Coombes which have lives of the saints in series.

There are also churches with wall paintings at:

Eastbourne: Rotherfield   Weymouth: Cerne Abbas
Deal or Dover: Barfreston   Poole: Cranbourne
Caister: Hemblington   Hartlepool: Pittington
Folkestone: Newington   Penzance: Breaze
Isle of Wight: Shorwell and Godshill

These are only examples; a little research in your local library will reveal others. These are also worth a visit:

Peakirk in Cambridgeshire   Charlwood in Surrey
Corby Glen in Lincolnshire   Stoke Dry in Leicestershire
Fairstead in Essex   East Wellow in Hampshire

And there are many others. Has your own town or village an old parish church with a wall painting? There is one at the old Norman church of St Nicholas, less than one mile from where I am writing.

Stained-glass window

Some beautiful stained glass still remains from the Middle Ages, but not much. Those opposed to Catholicism deliberately smashed most of it. This was especially true of the period of Cromwell and the Puritans. But it is still very worthwhile for the family to go out of its way to look for the early glass with its Bible stories and pictures of the saints. The best glass is to be found in the cathedrals of Canterbury, Lincoln and York Minster. Among a number of other places, very old stained glass can be found in the parish churches at the following:

> Brabourne and Westwell in Kent
> Madley and Fladbury in Herefordshire
> Stanton Harcourt and Horspath in Oxfordshire
> Harlow and Margaretting in Essex
> Brampton and Doddiscombsleigh in Devon
> St Kew and St Neots in Cornwall
> Minster and Selby Abbey in North Yorkshire
> Trysull and Okeover in Staffordshire

And in Ely Cathedral there is the Stained Glass Museum, in the North Triforium.

While you are in these old parish churches, look out for other points of interest, for example the Saxon and Norman fonts that can still be found in some places.

A 'saints' project

Children usually enjoy learning about the saints. Try having them make a scrap book each, and challenge them to find out all they can about saints, the only limitation being that *all* the material – drawings of wall pictures, information about stained-glass windows, etc. – must come from inside old churches (libraries are not allowed!).

It is an old Catholic tradition to name children after canonised saints so that the child has a heavenly patron throughout life. Most Catholic parents still follow this custom although they may well have chosen the name because they like the sound of it or because it is popular in the family. While they are not likely to think about it very often, it is good for the children to know a little about the saint whose name they have been given. Each saint has a special feast-day (although not all of these are shown on the Church's calendar) and this can be kept each year by the family.

The family's own calendar
Every Catholic has three days in the year which call for personal celebration. The first is the one that everyone remembers – the birthday; the second is the anniversary-day of christening and the third is the feast-day of the patron saint. So an imaginary little boy called Peter might have his birthday on 18 February, his christening day anniversary on 28 March and his feast day on 29 June: three days each year to recall and celebrate.

In a family of five people there will be a total of fifteen days each year to remember. These can be worked out and entered on the calendar that most families have hanging in the kitchen. The dates of the children's baptisms will be on their certificates and, with a little help from the local library, the school or the parish priest, you will be able to discover the dates of the patron saints' feast-days.

It is a good idea to make a separate and special 'family celebration calendar'. One way to do this is to get a large sheet of paper and make a list of dates, allowing a big border round the edge for the children to decorate. (They might like to use some of the symbols we spoke of earlier.) It can be arranged in date order or in columns like this:

	Birthday	*Baptismal Day*	*Saint's Day*
Mum	5 April	12 May	17 November
Dad	20 May	1 July	13 June
Helen	21 February	18 April	18 August
Peter	18 February	28 March	29 June
David	5 November	12 December	1 March

These special family days can be celebrated with an appropriate grace at mealtimes and the children might like to make a card to mark the day.

New beginnings

Before we arrive at the feast-day of all the saints (All Saints' Day), we have the 'back-to-school' month of September. Because there is a kind of new beginning in early September with the start of the new school year, with parish societies and groups opening up again after the summer break, it makes an ideal opportunity to make a new start in the family. (To make any real progress in our relationship with God, every opportunity for a renewal effort needs to be made the most of.)

It may be that you would like to begin saying grace at meal-times, or perhaps follow one or two of the ideas in this book. If you feel you need an opportunity to get things going, there are several natural starting points in the course of the year:

> the beginning of the new school year
> the first Sunday of Advent
> 1 January
> the beginning of Lent

– all 'new beginning' days, suitable occasions for making a fresh start.

October rosary

Each month in the Church's year is dedicated to a theme. The most significant are May, the month of Our Lady; June, dedicated to the Sacred Heart; October, dedicated to the rosary and November to the Holy Souls. Family prayer in October should include the rosary from time to time, if at all possible. There is no need to say more than the youngest member of the family can cope with.

November – month of the wider family

November brings a reminder that we are all members of the same very large family. We know well enough that at baptism we become children of God and members of the Christian family – God's own worldwide family. This is something we 'know' but only very rarely realise and recall. But November reminds us that the family not only reaches over national boundaries but also beyond the grave. The saints in heaven and the holy souls in purgatory have faced the same challenge of living the life of love we now face. They have struggled with their own self-love and have either courageously won or have needed their love purified before they could have union with 'Love' itself. With the saints and the souls in purgatory, we share the same baptism and the same calling. On 1 November we recall the saints, whether officially canonised or not, and ask them to pray for us, as we make our own pilgrimage through life. On the next day, and throughout November, we remember the souls of the departed and pray they will soon be released from their purification and united with our loving Father.

HALLOWE'EN

You can't miss All Saints' Day (or All Hallows as it was once called) because it is the only holy day in the year announced by all the children and proclaimed by an evening based on pagan superstition. In early medieval times the evening of All Hallows was a special holy time of preparation for the next day's feast. In the Celtic and Anglo-Saxon period the same date was the day before the start of their New Year. It was an occasion to placate the spirits of the dead and drive away evil spirits. The pagan goings-on on that day so heavily influenced the Christian festival of All Hallows Eve that gradually the religious connection was lost.

Irish immigrants introduced the idea to the United States. The Americans loved it and the customs of the evening were developed. Through the years, it has become an evening of fun and an opportunity to dress up. No harm is done provided there is no sign of the children taking it too seriously, or the very young and sensitive being alarmed and frightened by the masks and ghoulish attire.

ALL SAINTS' DAY

This day cannot pass without a special grace or table prayer. It is also a good opportunity to display in the kitchen, or around the house, any pictures from the summer research on saints. If the children have statues or pictures of their own patron saints they might like to arrange a few flowers in front of them as a mark of love and respect.

CHRIST THE KING

We end the Church's year on a note of confidence and triumph. Jesus is alive and with us; he lives by faith in our hearts. We belong to him and he belongs to us. He is our king.

Time has caught up with us again but we need never fear its passing. Christ our King is Lord of time and love. Our whole year has been passed in the light of one day – Easter Sunday – which alone ties together and makes sense of everything we have tried to do.

The children can be reminded today of the visit to the stable of the Magi (or kings) and of how, with their gifts, they foretold that Jesus would be a king. We can also draw the children's attention to the 'O' antiphon which proclaims Jesus 'King of the Nations' (see page 21). If an opportunity arises, that prayer could be used today. As this feast-day always comes on a Sunday, the last Sunday of the Church's year, it is not difficult to make something of Sunday teatime, perhaps to bake a crown cake (described on page 36). At that meal, or at Sunday dinner, the grace could be a special one; something like this:

> Almighty Father, every day
> we pray that your kingdom may come.
> We believe that Jesus, our risen Lord,
> lives by faith in our hearts.

May he reign there as king
and may his kingdom come in this home and family.
We thank you now for this food
which we are about to share.
May we be always grateful for your fatherly care. Amen.

The coming of love

Next Sunday is the first Sunday of Advent, when we start the Church's year all over again. In the next seven days we need to think about the Advent wreath, the Advent calendar, resolutions perhaps, and so on. But what we really require is a deep realisation of our daily need for love and of how Love himself is always longing to come and be one with us.

INDEX

Abstinence	50	Coming, the	13
Advent	10, 13-26	Communion of Saints	105
Advent blessing	23	Community of love	11
Advent calendar	15	Confession	49
Advent candle	18	Confirmation	89-91
Advent House	21	Converts	89
Advent resolutions	14	Creation	11, 13
Advent wreath	16-18	Crown	36
All Saints	104, 106	Crucifix	66
All Souls	104		
Altar	77	Death	65
Angels	43	Dove	86
Ascension Day	79	Dressing up	35
Ash Wednesday	46, 57		
		Easter	7, 32, 45, 72-79, 96, 106
Baby	11, 27	Easter candle	73, 74
Baptism	38, 68	Easter cards	74
Baptism of Jesus	36	Easter decorations	72
Baptistery	38	Easter egg	74, 75
Bible	100	Easter tree	52
Birthday	31-32	Easter vigil	75, 90
Butterfly	78	Epiphany	34
		Epiphany blessing	36
CAFOD	50	Eucharist	49, 68
Calendar, family	103	Example	56
Candles	88		
Cathedral	98	Faith	39
Christ the King	106	Family	95
Christian Unity	40	Family fast day	50
Christmas	27	Family prayers	57
Christmas cards	28	Father Christmas	24
Christmas crib	29-30	Fire	86
Christmas decorations	28	Fish	50
Christmas gifts	31	Fonts	102
Christmas tree	22	Formal prayers	59
Church	85	Fridays	49, 50

Gifts	31	'O' prayers	19
Good Friday	55, 69	October Rosary	104
Grace	57, 58	Our Father	62
Hail Mary	62	Passion	71
Hallowe'en	105	Passover	67
Holiday	96	Patron saints	103
Holiness	95	Pentecost	81, 84-88
Holy Communion	69	Phoenix	78
Holy Family	33	Posture	61
Holy Souls	105	Prayer	55, 58-64
Holy Week	54	Prayer, homes, centres of	8
Hot cross buns	70	Procession of witness	71
Jesse Tree	21-23	Reconciliation	48
John the Baptist	37	Resolutions	47
		Resurrection	7, 65, 70, 78, 96
Kings	30, 35-36	Rosary	62
Lamb	79	Sacraments	91
Language	82	St Nicholas' Day	24
Lent	44, 64	Saints	97, 100
Liturgy	97	Saints' Days	103
Life	9, 28	Santa Claus	24
Lord's Prayer	62	Self-discipline	43
Love	10, 11, 13, 28, 84, 95, 97	Self-knowledge	47
		Self-love	42
		Self-preservation	42
Magi	30, 35-36	Sexual expression	11
Marriage	11, 95	Sharing	42
Mary	63, 92	Stations of the Cross	51, 70
Mass	77	Stained glass	102
Maturity	13	Sunday	49, 77
Maundy Thursday	68	Sunday meal	77
Memorare	62	Symbolism	78
Missionaries	85, 89		
Mothering Sunday	54	Table prayers	50, 58
		Teenagers	56, 63, 79, 96
Night prayers	59	Time	9, 13, 27, 95, 96

Toy service	25	Week of prayer	40
Twelve days of Christmas	32	Whitsun	85
		Witness	71
Wall paintings	100		
Way of the cross	51, 70	Year, Church's	10, 107